Jessie Snyder

make it yourself

The Complete Step-by-Step Library of Needlework and Crafts

COLUMBIA HOUSE/New York

Editor: Mary Harding
Assistant Editor: Margo Coughtrie
Editorial Assistant: Sally Fisher
Consultants: Greta Barrett/Angela Jeffs (Sewing)/
Patsy North (Embroidery and Crafts)/
Frances Rogers (Knitting and Crochet)
Managing Editor: Nicholas Wright
Design Co-ordinators: David Harper/Jan Browne
Production Control: Frank Sloan
Editorial Director: Graham Donaldson

Distributed by Columbia House, 51 West 52nd Street, New York, New York 10019

Introduction

Now is when the real fun begins. Once you have learned the basic techniques, you will have the confidence and competence to try the endless variety of designs and patterns which make needlework and crafts so popular. And you will discover the great satisfaction that comes from making something yourself.

Also, you will now appreciate the savings that come from making your own clothes and home accessories because you can create custom designs which you could never afford to buy. You will have the flexibility to adapt the designs and colors to your own needs and you can ensure that the quality of workmanship and materials which make today's "good" clothes and home furnishings so expensive.

In this and the following volumes, there are projects to delight and challenge you as your skills increase. The designs range from the very practical to the purely decorative to the amusing and superfluous. The complete series gives you a wide range of distinctive fashions and accessories for you and the whole family, plus countless ideas which will add a unique and personal touch to your home decorating.

We have filled these volumes with new and exciting things to make—the rest is up to you.

make it yourself

Contents   Page

How to use this book...

Selecting a yarn

In this series, we are introducing a new and easy way to identify the yarn used in our knitting and crochet features! You will find an actual-size, colored photograph of the yarn given with each set of directions.

Materials Required:

150 (200) gm or 6 (7) oz each of yellow and green, 50 gm or 2 oz blue [100 gm = 360 m or 390 yds]. Knitting needles size 4 (Am) or 10 (Eng).

At one time or another, you have probably suffered the disappointment of finding that the yarn specified in knitting and crochet directions is difficult to obtain or totally unavailable in your area. When this happens you are faced with the often impossible task of finding a substitute yarn. By matching a yarn against our photograph, you can choose a yarn of similar weight and texture from the range of yarns available in your store or favorite needlework shop.

This method is also helpful if you have yarn left over from other projects and you are unsure whether it is the proper weight or texture and whether you have sufficient yardage to finish a new shawl or pullover.

To help you determine the amount of yarn needed, we have also listed the yardage per skein for the yarn used. Most yarn companies give the yardage per skein in their sample books, and many shops have interchangeable yarn lists which give the yardages per unit weight. You will then be able to see whether you will need to make adjustments in the number of skeins required of the yarn which you have chosen.

Before you start to work the patter work a test swatch and match against the Tension given in th directions (see the Tension Gaug instructions below). Adjust th needle or hook size if necessar Any yarn which can be worked the tension given in the directio can be used for that pattern.

Centimeters or inches?

The metric system of measureme is gaining greater use and accep ance, and some needlework ar crafts equipment and materials a already sold by the metric weigl and/or length. For your co venience, we have given all th weights and measures in bot systems. NOTE: In some cases, th conversions are not exact. Th measurements have been rounde to the nearest convenient appropriate number.

Tension gauge

One key to successful knitting or crocheting is the tension! Each of our directions is based on the given tension gauge (number of rows and stitches to 10 cm or 4").
To check your tension, work a test piece 12 cm or 5" square in the stitch pattern. Make a cardboard template with a 10 cm or 4" square cut out of it. Place the template over your swatch and count the rows and stitches. Compare the numbers with the tension gauge given in the directions. If your swatch has too few stitches and rows, work more tightly or use smaller equipment. If you have more than the number given, use larger needles, or hook. Directions for the items shown can be used for any yarn of similar thickness and texture, providing you can achieve the proper tension.
Do not be upset if you find that you do have to adjust the needle or hook size. This does not mean that there is anything wrong with your knitting or crocheting. The needle and hook sizes given in the directions are an average, but by no means an absolute. There is great variation in the tension at which different people work, and you will even find slight variations in the tension of your work. On days when you are ten or tired, your knitting or crochetir will probably be a little tighter.

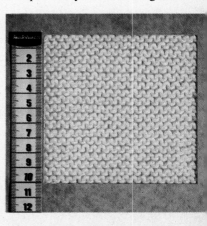

fashion sizing

ressmaking
o you know your size? Don't just ıy 'yes', because as you already now, the fit of pattern and ready-›-wear sizes varies.
o eliminate confusion, we have ttered our sizes (A, B, C) instead f giving them the traditional umbering (10, 12).
emeasure yourself and match your-ody measurements with those iven in the chart below. All of the atterns are designed according to hese measurements, so choose the attern size which is right for your neasurements. You may have to nake minor adjustments in the attern pieces to adapt them to our body contours, and Dress-naking Pattern Sheet 2 explains ıow to do this. Other dressmaking ›attern sheets will deal with more omplex fitting for specific garments uch as pants.
)O NOT MEASURE THE ATTERNS. Every pattern includes, ccording to the design, an added neasure to allow for easy movement vhen wearing the garment. Just ompare your body measurements vith the measurements given in the hart and choose the proper size.
Each pattern is given in five sizes. Two of the sizes are given on the pattern sheet and the other three sizes can be easily drawn from the two sizes given. Directions for adapting for the three additional sizes are given on each pattern sheet. Even if you are not one of the standard pattern sizes, but are a mixed size made up of several standard measurements, you can still use our patterns. Since each pattern can be adapted for five sizes – a size smaller, a size larger, and a size between the two sizes actually marked on the pattern sheet – it is possible to construct a pattern for yourself. Directions for constructing a mixed-size pattern are given on Dressmaking Pattern Sheet 2.

Knitting and Crochet
The knitting and crochet sizes are based on the Dressmaking Body Measurements Chart. For each direction, you will be given the actual body measurements for which the garment is intended. The finished knitted or crocheted garment will be larger than the given measurements to allow for comfort and movement.

Size: Directions are for 92 cm (36″) bust. Changes for 96, 100 cm (37½″, 39½″) bust are in brackets.

Do you know your size?

Don't just say 'yes'. Remeasure yourself, following the diagrams and instructions, and then check the Body Measurements chart.

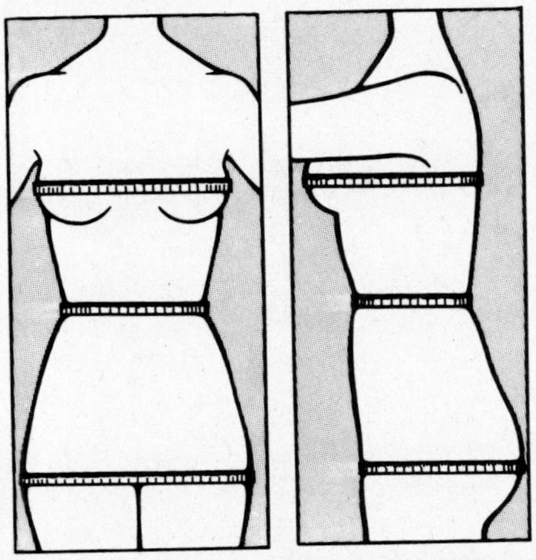

Bust – measure around the fullest part of the bust.
Waist – tie a string around your body so that it settles comfortably at your natural waistline. Measure your waist at the string.
Hips – measure around the fullest part of your hips (this generally falls 7″–9″ below your waistline).
Important hints:
When taking measurements, do not hold the tape measure slack or pull it too tight. The tape must lie evenly horizontal all around the body – it should not go up at the back and down at the front. You will find it simpler and more accurate to be measured by someone else.

Body measurements chart

WOMEN

Size	A	B	C	D	E	F	G	H
Bust	80 cm (31½″)	84 cm (33″)	88 cm (34½″)	92 cm (36″)	96 cm (37½″)	100 cm (39½″)	104 cm (41″)	108 cm (42½″)
Waist	59 cm (23¼″)	63.5 cm (25″)	68 cm (26½″)	72.5 cm (28½″)	77 cm (30½″)	81.5 cm (32″)	86 cm (34″)	90 cm (35½″)
Hips	86 cm (34″)	90 cm (35½″)	94 cm (37″)	98 cm (38½″)	102 cm (40″)	106 cm (42″)	110 cm (43½″)	114 cm (45″)

MEN

Size	J	K	L	M	N	O	P	Q
Chest	84 cm (33″)	88 cm (34½″)	92 cm (36″)	96 cm (37½″)	100 cm (39½″)	104 cm (41″)	108 cm (42½″)	112 cm (44″)
Hip	88 cm (34½″)	92 cm (36″)	96 cm (37½″)	100 cm (39½″)	104 cm (41″)	108 cm (42½″)	112 cm (44″)	116 cm (45½″)
Neck	36 cm (14″)	37 cm (14½″)	38 cm (15″)	39 cm (15½″)	40 cm (15¾″)	41 cm (16″)	42 cm (16½″)	43 cm (17″)
Arm	60 cm (23¾″)	61 cm (24″)	62 cm (24¼″)	63 cm (24¾″)	64 cm (25¼″)	65 cm (25½″)	66 cm (26″)	67 cm (26½″)

CHILDREN

Size	S	T	U	V	W	X	Y	Z
Height	110 cm (43″)	116 cm (45½″)	122 cm (48″)	128 cm (50½″)	134 cm (52¾″)	140 cm (55″)	146 cm (57½″)	152 cm (60″)
Chest	60 cm (23¾″)	62 cm (24¼″)	64 cm (25¼″)	66 cm (26″)	68 cm (26¾″)	70 cm (27½″)	73 cm (28¾″)	76 cm (29¾″)
Waist	58 cm (23″)	59 cm (23¼″)	60 cm (23¾″)	61 cm (24″)	62 cm (24¼″)	63 cm (24¾″)	64 cm (25¼″)	65 cm (25¾″)
Hips	66 cm (26″)	68 cm (26¾″)	70 cm (27½″)	72 cm (28¼″)	74 cm (29″)	76 cm (29¾″)	80 cm (31½″)	84 cm (33″)

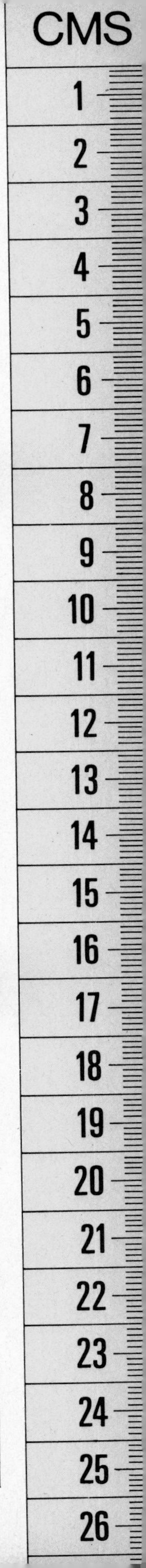

Patterned in a blue mood

Size: Directions are for 80 cm (31½″) bust. Changes for 88 cm (34½″) bust are in brackets.

Materials Required:

350 (400) gm or 13 (15) oz pale blue [100 gm = 360 m or 390 yds]. Knitting needles and a circular needle size 2 (Am) or 11 (Eng). Stitch holder.

Stitch Pattern 1 (for Back): Stocking or stockinette stitch.

Stitch Pattern 2 (for edgings and Sleeves): K 1, P 1 rib.

Stitch Pattern 3 (for Front): See chart. R 1–14 make one pattern.

Tension: For Stitch Pattern 1: 25 sts and 38 R = 10 cm or 4″. For Stitch Pattern 3: 25 sts and 36 R = 10 cm or 4″.

Abbreviations: St(s) = stitch(es). R = row(s). K = knit. P = purl. Sl = slip.

DIRECTIONS

Back: Cast on 107 (115) sts and work 12 cm or 4¾″ in Stitch Pattern 2. Then in Stitch Pattern 1, work straight until piece is 33 (32) cm or 13″ (12½″).

The pattern repeat begins here.

Shape Armholes: Cast off 3 sts at beginning of next 2 R, 2 sts at beginning of next 4 R, then decrease 1 st each end of next 7 R – 79 (87) sts. Work until Back is 50 cm or 19½".

Shape Neck and Shoulders: Cast off center 39 (41) sts, then work on sts on one side. At shoulder edge, cast off 3 sts at beginning of every 2nd R 5 times (3 sts 2 times, 4 sts 3 times). *At the same time,* at the neck edge cast off 2 sts at beginning of every 2nd R 2 times, then decrease 1 st 1 time. Work other side to match.

Front: Cast on 107 (115) sts and work 12 cm or 4¾" in Stitch Pattern 2. P the next R. Change to Stitch Pattern 3 as shown in chart, working an edge st at each end and purling the even R. For small size, work Right Repeat 7 times, the Middle 1 time, and Left Repeat 7 times. For large size, begin Right Repeat at arrow, then work Right Repeat 7 times, Middle 1 time, Left Repeat 7 times, then work the 1st 4 sts of Left Repeat again. Note: In the 5th R, the sts before and after the edge sts are K 1 instead of make 1. Work all other sts as given in the chart. Repeat the chart until piece measures same as Back to armholes. Keeping continuity of pattern, shape armholes as for Back; work straight to 40 cm or 15¾".

Shape Neck and Shoulders: Cast off center 21 (23) sts,

then work on sts on 1 side. At neck edge cast off 2 sts at beginning of every 2nd R 3 times, decrease 1 st 4 times, then decrease 1 st in every 4th R 4 times. *At the same time,* at 50 cm or 19½" at shoulder edge cast off 3 sts at beginning of every 2nd R 5 times (3 sts 2 times, 4 sts 3 times). Work other side to match.

Sleeves: Cast on 46 (54) sts and work in Stitch Pattern 2, increasing 1 st each end of every 10th R until there are 72 (80) sts. Work until piece is 45 cm or 17¾".

Shape Top: Cast off 3 sts at beginning of next 2 R, 2 sts at beginning of next 2 (6) R, decrease 1 st each end of next 21 (18) R, cast off 2 sts at beginning of next 2 (4) R, and 3 sts at beginning of next 2 R. Cast off remaining 10 (12) sts.

Finishing: Press lightly (do not press ribbing). Join shoulders. Using circular needle, pick up 140 (146) sts around neck and work Stitch Pattern 2 for 3 cm or 1¼". Cast off. Sew seams.

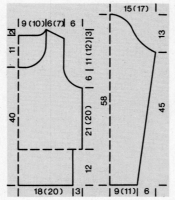

◀ Half-patterns for small (large) sizes. Measurements are in centimeters, inches are given in the directions.

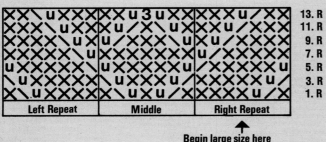

◀ Follow chart for Stitch Pattern 3. The odd-numbered rows are knitted and the even-numbered rows are purled.

Left Repeat | Middle | Right Repeat

13. R
11. R
9. R
7. R
5. R
3. R
1. R

Begin large size here

X = Knit

\ = Slip 1, knit 1, pass slipped st over

/ = Knit 2 sts together

u = Increase (pass yarn over)

3 = Work point on 3 sts (See How-to)

Knitted lace designs are made by increasing and decreasing stitches to create a pattern of open and solid areas. It is important to maintain a balance between the increased and decreased stitches so that the overall number of stitches in each row is the same. This pattern is made with slanted decrease and increasing by passing the yarn over the needle.

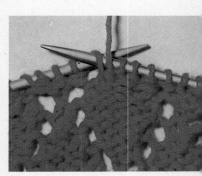

1 To purl across the increase stitches in the even numbered row, insert needle as for a purl stitch.

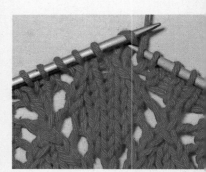

1 Increase one stitch. Insert needle into next stitch as if to knit and slip it onto the right needle.

Increasing a stitch to create a space

1 To increase a stitch, pass the yarn over the right needle from the front to the back.

2 To create a space on the right, pass yarn over needle and then work a slanted decrease to the left.

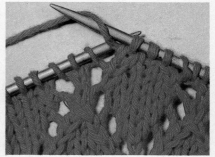

3 To create a space on the left, work a slanted decrease to the right and then pass yarn over needle.

Working across an increased stitch

Pass the yarn under the needle and purl the stitch. The increased stitch creates a space.

3 If working on a circular needle, knit the even numbered rows and insert the needle as for a knit stitch.

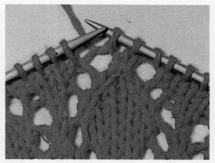

4 Pass the yarn under the needle and knit the stitch. The increased stitch creates a space.

Forming a point with left and right decrease

Knit the next two stitches on the needle together to form a slanted decrease to the right.

3 Lift the slipped-stitch over the stitch formed by the two stitches knitted together.

4 This forms a slanted decrease to the left. To balance the number of stitches, increase another stitch.

Three-dimensional
design creates a

Whipped cream coverlet

Size: 130 x 240 cm (51" x 94½").

Materials Required:

2700 gm or 96 oz white. 5 double-pointed needles size 2 (Am) or 11 (Eng).

Stitch Pattern: See chart.

Abbreviations: St(s) = stitch(es). R = row(s). K = knit. P = purl. Inc = increase. Rnd(s) = round(s).

DIRECTIONS

For the bedspread you will require 45 squares and 22 triangles.

Squares: Each square is worked in rnds on 5 double-pointed needles. The chart gives ¼ of the square, so the pattern must be repeated 4 times in each rnd. Follow the chart for the odd-numbered rnds and knit every even-numbered rnd, working the 1st st of each repeat in twisted knit stitch. Cast on 8 sts, placing 2 sts on each of 4 needles. Work Rnds 1–48, then P 2 rnds. Cast off.

Triangles: Cast on 7 sts. Work back and forth across the rows. Work the odd-numbered R from the chart, beginning each R with an edge st, then working the pattern 2 times, and ending with a K st and an edge st. P the even-numbered R, working twisted purl st into the twisted knit sts.

Border: Cast on 9 sts. R 1: K 1, *inc 1, K 2 together in

twisted knit st, repeat from * 3 times. R 2 and all even-numbered R: K 1, inc 1, K to end. R 3: K 2, then repeat from * of R 1. R 5: K 3, then repeat from * of R 1. Continue thus until there are 16 sts. Next even R: Work as for R 2. Next odd R: Cast off 7 sts, K to end. Continue to repeat from R 1 until the work measures 7.5 m or 8¼ yds. Cast off.

Finishing: Pin out the squares and triangles, cover with a damp cloth, press lightly, and leave to dry. Join on wrong side with backstitch. Begin at lower edge by sewing 3 squares in between 4 triangles, then add 4 and 3 squares alternately to end. Sew 4 triangles at the other end and 7 triangles along each side. When all squares and triangles have been joined, sew on the border neatly.

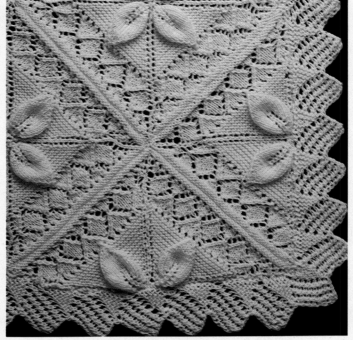

Patterned motifs are joined for the coverlet and a border finishes the edge.

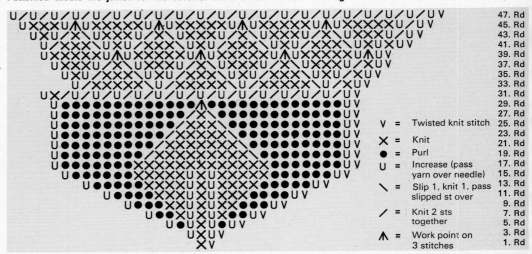

V =	Twisted knit stitch
X =	Knit
● =	Purl
U =	Increase (pass yarn over needle)
\ =	Slip 1, knit 1, pass slipped st over
/ =	Knit 2 sts together
⋀ =	Work point on 3 stitches

47. Rd
45. Rd
43. Rd
41. Rd
39. Rd
37. Rd
35. Rd
33. Rd
31. Rd
29. Rd
27. Rd
25. Rd
23. Rd
21. Rd
19. Rd
17. Rd
15. Rd
13. Rd
11. Rd
9. Rd
7. Rd
5. Rd
3. Rd
1. Rd

Pattern repeat: Each symbol represents one stitch of the odd-numbered rows. See the directions for the even rows.

A soft glow for evening

The metallic yarn creates a shimmery glow for the at-home hostess or the girl about town. The vertical ribs are flattering and texture contrast velvet pants a long skirt.

Size: Directions are for 84 cm (33") bust. Changes for 92 cm (36") bust are in brackets.

Materials Required:

350 (400) gm or 13 (15) oz grey. Knitting needles and a circular needle size 4 (Am) or 9 (Eng). 6 buttons.

Basic Pattern: K 4, P 4.
Border Rib: K 2, P 2.
Tension: 24 sts and 40 R = 10 cm or 4".
Abbreviations: St(s) = stitch(es). R = row(s). K = knit. P = purl.

DIRECTIONS

Back: With knitting needles cast on 110 (118) sts and work in Basic Pattern with edge st — R 1: K 1, *K 4, P 4. Repeat from * to last 5 sts, K 5. R 2: K 1, *P4, K 4. Repeat from * to last 5 sts, P 4, K 1. Continue straight until piece measures 8 cm or 3", then decrease 1 st at each end of next and every 8th R 6 times — 96 (104) sts. Work straight until piece measures 27 cm or 10½", then increase 1 st each end of the next and every 14th R 5 times — 106 (114) sts. Work straight until piece measures 47 cm or 18½".

Shape Armholes: Cast off 3 sts at beginning of next 2 R, 2 sts at beginning of next 4 R, then decrease 1 st each end of every R 7 times — 78 (86) sts. Continue straight until work measures 65 (66) cm or 25½" (26").

Shape Shoulders: Cast off center 32 sts for Neck edge in next R. Working on sts at one side, at Armhole edge, cast off 4 (5) sts at beginning of next R, in every 2nd R 5 (6) sts 2 times, 6 (7) sts 1 time. *At the same time,* at Neck edge, cast off 2 sts 1 time, 1 st 1 time. Work other side to match.

Left Front: Cast on 54 (58) sts and work in Basic

Pattern with edge st, shaping side, armhole, and shoulder as for Back. *At the same time,* at 40 cm or 15¾" decrease 1 st at neck edge alternately every 5th and 6th R 19 times.

Right Front: Work to match other front, reversing shapings.

Sleeves: Cast on 54 (62) sts and work in Basic Pattern as for Back, increasing 1 st each end of every 14th R 12 times — 78 (86) sts. Continue straight until sleeve measures 45 cm or 17¾".

Shape Top: Cast off 5 sts at beginning of next 2 R, 2 sts at beginning of next 4 (6) R. Decrease 1 st at each end of next 20 (18) R, 2 sts at beginning of next 4 (6) R, 3 sts at beginning of next 2 R. Cast off remaining 10 (14) sts.

Finishing: Press lightly. Join shoulders; sew in sleeves. Sew sleeve and side seams.

Front Border: With circular needle pick up 114 sts along right Front edge, 79 sts to Shoulder, 48 sts across Back Neck, 79 sts down Left edge and 114 sts to lower edge — 434 sts. Work back and forth in Border Rib, with chain stitch edge at each end for 3 cm or 1¼" ending at Right Front edge. Beginning 4 sts from end, work 6 buttonholes over 3 sts at 6 cm or 2½" intervals.

Horizontal rib border is knitted on.

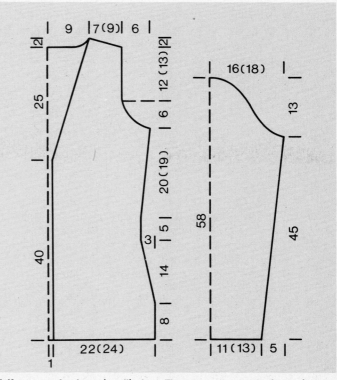

Half-patterns for large (small) sizes. The measurements are in centimeters.

Size: Directions are for 62 cm or 24½" chest. Changes for 66 cm or 26" chest are in brackets.

Materials Required:

200 (250) gm or 8 (9) oz in a brown mixture. Knitting needles size 4 (Am) or 9 (Eng). Stitch holder. 7 buttons. Cable needle.

Basic Pattern: R 1: K 1, *cross 2 sts to left (sl 1 st on cable needle and leave at front, K 1, sl the st on cable needle to right needle), K 4, cross 2 sts to right (sl 1 st on cable needle at back of work, sl next st on to right needle, K st from cable needle), P 2. Repeat from * to last st, K 1. R 2 and even-numbered R: K 1, *K 2, P 8, repeat from * to last st, K 1. R 3: K 1, *K 1, cross 2 sts to left, K 2, cross 2 sts to right, K 1, P 2, repeat from * to last st, K 1. R 5: K 1, * K2, cross 2 sts to left, cross 2 sts to right, K 2, P 2, repeat from * to last st, K 1. R 7: K 1, *K 3, cross the 2nd slipped st to right, K 3, P 2, repeat from * to last st, K 1. R 9: K 1, *K 2, cross 2 sts to right, cross 2 sts to left, K 2, P 2. Repeat from * to last st, K 1. R 11: K 1, *K 1, cross 2 sts to right, K 2, cross 2 sts to left, K 1, P 2, repeat from * to last st, K 1. R 13: K 1, *cross 2 sts to right, K 4, cross 2 sts to left, P 2, repeat from * to last st, K 1.

Tension: 27 sts and 34 R = 10 cm or 4" (with work slightly stretched).

Abbreviations: K = knit. P = purl. St(s) = stitch(es). Sl = slip. R = row.

DIRECTIONS

Begin at Left Sleeve. Cast on 42 (50) sts and work 5 cm or 2" in K 2, P 2 rib.
Next R: P 1 (4), *P twice into next st, P 1, repeat from * to last 1 (2) sts, P 1 (2). Work in Basic Pattern on these 62 (72) sts, increasing 1 st each end of every 8th (9th) R 9 times — 80 (90) sts. Continue to 30 (33) cm or 11" (12").
Shape Sides: Increase 1 st each end of next and every 2nd R, 2 sts at beginning of next 6 R, 5 sts on next 4 R, then cast on 22 (27) sts on next 2 R. Work straight to 45 (49) cm or 17¾" (19¼"), ending after wrong side R, then place 80 (90) sts on stitch holder for Back. Cast off next 9 sts; work remaining sts.
Now cast off 2 sts at neck edge of next 3 R, then decrease 1 st on next 3 neck edge R. Work on remaining 62 (72) sts to 48 (52) cm or 19 (20½"). Cast off.
Begin at center front for

The ribbed collar can be buttoned up and turned over for extra warmth.

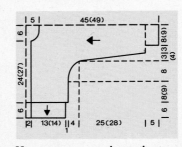

The front and lower borders are worked in rib to match the collar.

Measurements are in centimeters; inches are given in the directions.

other half. Cast on 62 (72) sts and work to match pattern to end of neck shaping, increasing at beginning of right side R. Increase 1 st on next 3 neck edge R, then 2 sts 3 times and 9 sts 1 time, then work to neck edge; place sts on stitch holder.
Go back to 80 (90) Back sts and work straight for 10 cm or 4", ending at neck edge. Work across Front sts on st holder. Continue other side to match, reversing shapings. End sleeve after a wrong side R. Work cuff decrease R: K 1 (4), *K 2 together, K 1. Repeat from * to last 1 (2) sts, K 1 (2). Work cuff rib, decreasing 20 (22) sts. Join side and sleeve seams. With right side facing, pick up 148 (156) sts all around lower edge and work 6 cm or 2¼" in K 2, P 2 rib. Cast off in rib.
For Right Front, pick up 72 (84) sts along edge and work in K 2, P 2 rib for 4 cm or 1½". Cast off in rib. Work Left Front to match, working 5 buttonholes in the 2nd R. Place the 1st one 2 cm or ¾" from lower edge and 4 more at 5 (6) cm or 2" (2¼") intervals by casting off 2 sts at these positions, then casting on 2 sts in next R.
For Neck Border, pick up 80 sts around neck and top of borders. Work in rib with 6th buttonhole on next R and 7th one at 5 (6) cm or 2" (2¼") interval. Continue straight to 8 cm or 3¼", then increase 1 st on alternate K ribs. When work is 10 cm or 4", increase in K ribs not increased in before. Work straight to 13 cm or 5". Cast off. Add buttons.

Criss-cross stitches for a criss-cross pattern

ssed slip stitches
ate a diamond pattern
elief. The cardigan
knitted in one piece
m cuff to cuff so
t the wide ribs form
rizontal pattern strips.

Slip-stitch patterns

Many pattern variations can be achieved with slip stitches. When worked in a vertical row, a raised stripe effect is produced. Diagonal lines are made with crossed slip stitches; diamonds and zigzags are made with intersecting lines of crossed slip stitches. The slipped stitches create a pattern in relief.

A vertical slip-stitch pattern

1 Insert the right needle into the front of the stitch on the left needle from right to left. Slip the stitch onto the right needle.

2 The yarn is at the back of the piece and the stitches between the slipped stitches are worked as knit stitches.

3 This is what the piece looks like on the reverse side. Both the knitted and the slipped stitches are purled in the purl row.

A crossed slip-stitch pattern

1 Crossing a slip stitch from left to right: Place the stitch which will lie underneath on a spare needle at the back of the piece.

2 Slip the following stitch onto the right needle. With the yarn at the back of the piece, knit the stitch held on the spare needle.

3 Crossing a slip stitch from right to left: Place the stitch which will lie on top on a spare needle at the front of the piece.

4 Knit the following stitch, then slip the stitch held on the spare needle onto the right needle to slant the slipped stitch to the right.

Horizontal and vertical buttonholes

Horizontal buttonhole

1 Cast off the number of stitches given in the directions or the number to fit your button. <u>Note:</u> if the last stitch is a purl stitch, do not cast it off.

2 Slip the last purl stitch of the buttonhole area back onto the left needle and knit it together with the next stitch to decrease one stitch.

3 In the next row, cast on the same number of stitches as you cast off or decreased in the last row. Do not make the cast-on stitches too loose.

Vertical buttonhole

1 Divide the stitches in the center of the border and work the stitches at the outside edge of the buttonhole to the proper height.

2 When one side of the buttonhole is finished, work the rest of the piece to the same height to complete the buttonhole on the other side.

3 Close the end of the buttonhole by working across all of the stitches on both sides of the buttonhole, beginning the row at edge of piece.

For spring or autumn
Versatile tweed jacket

This comfortable multi-season jacket is quickly made with two strands of yarn and large needles. The long line looks equally smart with skirts or pants.

Knitting

A plain color emphasizes the varied thickness of the yarn.

Yarn made of a two-color mixture produces a tweed effect.

...ze: Directions are for a ...cm or 33″ bust. Changes ... a 92 cm or 36″ bust ...e in brackets.

...aterials Required:

...00 (1300) gm or 39 (46) ... brown/white mixture ...0 gm = 65 m or 70 yds]. ...itting needles size 13 ...m) or 000 (Eng). 6 but-...ns. Stitch holders.

...asic Stitch: Stocking or ...ockinette stitch.

...roken Rib Pattern: ...1: *K 1, P 1, repeat from * ... last st, K 1. R 2 (right ...de): *P 1, K 1, repeat ...om * to last st, P 1. R 3: ...epeat R 2. R 4: Repeat ...1.

...ension: 8 sts and 13 R = ...0 cm or 4″, with yarn ...orked double.

...bbreviations: St(s) = ...itch(es). R = row(s). ... = knit. P = purl. St st = ...ocking or stockinette ...itch.

...IRECTIONS

...ack: Work with double ...rn throughout garment. ...ast on 39 (43) sts and ...ork 6 cm or 2½″ in Rib ...attern. Continue in st st ...nd when work measures ...0 cm or 4″, decrease 1 st ...ach end of next R and on ...llowing 18th R. Work on ...5 (39) sts to 49 (48) cm or ...9¼″ (18¾″).

...hape Armholes: Cast off ...sts at beginning of next ...R, 1 (2) sts at beginning ...f next 2 R. Work straight ...n 29 (31) sts to 72 cm or ...8¼″.

...hape Shoulders: Cast off ...sts at beginning of next ...R and 4 (5) sts at begin-...ing of next 2 armhole edge ... *At the same time*, at ...3 cm or 28¾″, cast off ...enter 9 sts, and 2 sts on ...ext neck edge R.

...ocket Linings (2 re-...quired): Cast on 12 (14) sts and work 18 cm or 7″ in st st, ending with P R. Place on st holder.

Right Front: Cast on 23 (25) sts and work 6 cm or 2½″ in Rib Pattern. Keep 6 sts in rib at Front edge, next 4 sts in st st and remaining sts in Rib Pattern. Work thus, shaping side to match Back. *At the same time*, at 16 cm or 6¼″ work 1st buttonhole over 3rd and 4th st of border and 5 more at 10 cm or 4″ inter-vals. When work measures 24 cm or 9½″, ending at side edge, make Pocket: P 1, cast off 12 (14) sts, P 4, work Rib Pattern on 6 sts. In next R, work over the 12 (14) sts of one Pocket Lining. Work in st st over main sts and keep 6 Front border sts in Rib Pattern. Shape Armhole to match Back at 49 (48) cm or 19¼″ (18¾″) and work to 68 cm or 26¾″. Place 6 border sts on st. holder, cast off 2 sts at next neck edge R, and shape shoulder at 72 cm or 28¼″ to match Back.

Left Front: Work to match Right Front, omitting buttonholes and reversing shapings.

Sleeves: Cast on 27 (31) sts and work 10 cm or 4″ in Rib Pattern, decreasing 1 st each end of last R − 25 (29) sts. Work straight, increas-ing 1 st each end at 20 cm or 8″ and each end of following 24th R − 29 (33) sts. Continue straight to 56 cm or 22″.

Shape Top: In every K R, cast off 2 sts at beginning of R and decrease 1 st at end 8 (9) times. Cast off remaining 5 (6) sts.

Belt: Cast on 7 sts and work in Rib Pattern for 120 cm or 47¼″. Cast off in rib.

Collar: Join shoulders. Work across 6 Right Front border sts, pick up 31 sts around neck, work across other border sts. Work in Rib Pattern for 22 cm or 8½″. Cast off in rib.

Finishing: Press. Sew in sleeves, then sew up sleeve and side seams, with 10 cm or 4″ of sleeve seam sewn on right side for turn-back cuff. Sew on buttons.

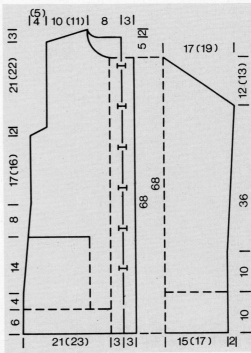

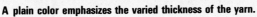

Half-pattern for small (large) sizes. The measurements are given in centimeters; inches are in the directions.

279

Great coat to knit at top speed

Quick-knit jacket is made on large needles with eight strands of yarn

Size: Directions are for 96 cm (37½") chest. Changes for 104 cm (41") chest are in brackets.

Materials Required:

1800 (2000) gm or 64 (71) oz beige [100 gm = 330 m or 360 yds]. Knitting needles size 15 (Am) or 000 (Eng). Stitch holders.

Basic Stitch: Stocking or stockinette stitch using 8 strands of yarn.

Border Pattern: Use 8 strands of yarn. R 1: Work K 1, P 1 rib. R 2: K the K sts and P the P sts. R 3: P the K sts and K the P sts. R 4: Repeat R 2. Repeat these 4 R.

Note: 8 strands are used throughout.

Tension: 7 sts and 10 R = 10 cm or 4".

Abbreviations: St(s) = stitch(es). St st = stocking or stockinette stitch. K = knit. P = purl. R = row(s).

DIRECTIONS

Back: Cast on 35 (38) sts and work in Border Pattern for 10 cm or 4". Change to St st and work straight until piece measures 70 cm or 27½", ending after a P R.

Shape Neck and Shoulders: Cast off 3 (4) sts at beginning of next 2 R — 29 (30) sts. Cast off the center 7 (6) sts and continue on sts at one side. Cast off 4 sts at the beginning of the next R and 2 sts at the beginning of the following R. Cast off remaining sts. Work other side to match.

Left Front: Cast on 22 (24) sts and work in Border Pattern for 10 cm or 4".

Next R: K to last 17 (19) sts, then work Border Pattern to end. Continue to work 5 sts up Front edge in

It has a big collar, big cuffs, big pockets, and a belt instead of buttons.

Border Pattern and rema[...]ing sts in St st until wo[...] measures 60 cm or 23-[...] ending at Front edge. Wo[...] 1 st from St st into Bord[...] Pattern in every 2nd R [...] times — 8 sts in Bord[...] Pattern and 14 (16) sts [...] St st. Work straight un[...] piece measures 68 cm [...] 26¾", ending at Front edg[...]

Shape Neck and Should[...] Next R: Work over 8 bord[...] sts and leave on stit[...] holder. Decrease 1 st [...] neck edge every 2nd R [...] times. *At the same tim[...]* when work measures sam[...] as Back to shoulder, [...] next 3 armhole edge [...] cast off 3 (4) sts, 4 (4) st[...] then 4 (5) sts.

Right Front: Work [...] match other Front, rever[...] shapings.

Sleeves: Cast on 35 s[...] and work in Border Patte[...] for 14 cm or 5½". Change [...] St st and decrease 1 st ea[...] end of every 2nd R 2 time[...] Continue straight on 31 s[...] until piece is 56 cm or 22[...]

Shape Shoulder: Cast off [...] sts at beginning of next [...] R, and 3 sts at beginnin[...] of next 4 R. Cast off [...] remaining sts.

Pockets (make 2): Cast o[...] 15 sts. Work Border Patter[...] for 20 cm or 8". Cast off.

Belt: Cast on 4 sts an[...] work in Border Pattern f[...] 180 cm or 70". Cast off.

Finishing: Join shoulder[...] With right side facing, pic[...] up 8 sts on stitch hold[...] at Right Front border, pic[...] up 32 sts around nec[...] then pick up Left Fron[...] border sts. Work in Borde[...] Pattern for 16 cm or 6¼[...] Cast off in rib.

Sew in sleeves, then se[...] up side and sleeve seam[...] making seam on right sid[...] for turn-back of cuff. Se[...] on pockets in positio[...] shown in photograph.

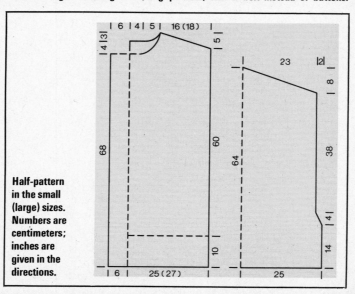

Half-pattern in the small (large) sizes. Numbers are centimeters; inches are given in the directions.

6 | 4 | 5 | 16 (18)
4 [3]
5
6 | 4 | 5
23 | 2|
68
60
64
8
38
10
14
6 | 25 (27)
25

Use eighteen subtle shades

Create an optical illusion

The zigzag of alternating light and dark stripes gives a three-dimensional effect.

The optical trick is simple. Diagonal stripes in light and dark shades of the same color are placed side by side in a zigzag pattern. Two shades of any color will produce the same effect.

Size: 130 x 225 cm (51$\frac{1}{4}$" x 88$\frac{1}{2}$").

Materials Required:

100 gm or 4 oz each of red, dark green, purple, blackberry, dark grey, blue, rust, burgundy, light burgundy, green, lilac, old rose, light grey, light blue, light brown, dark yellow, beige, pale yellow [50 gm = 188 m or 205 yds]. Knitting needles size 5 (Am) or 8 (Eng).

Basic Stitch: Stocking or stockinette stitch. The diagonal pattern is produced by increasing at one side and decreasing at the other side of the same R.

Color Sequence of Dark Stripes: 23 R light brown, *20 R each of dark yellow, red, burgundy, dark green, purple, blackberry, dark grey, blue, light brown, repeat from * 2 times, then work 23 R dark yellow.

Color Sequence of Light Stripes: 23 R beige, *20 R each of pale yellow, rust, light burgundy, green, lilac, old rose, light grey, light blue, beige, repeat from * 2 times, then work 23 R pale yellow.

Tension: 23 sts and 34 R = 10 cm or 4".

Abbreviations: St(s) = stitch(es). R = row(s). K = knit. P = purl.

DIRECTIONS

Dark Stripes (5 required): Using light brown, cast on 40 sts and K 3 R.

R 4: Work in front and back of next st, then K to last 3 sts, slip 1, K 1, pass slip st over, K 1. **R 5:** P.

Repeat these 2 R until 23 R of light brown have been worked. Continue in Color Sequence, working 20 R in each color. When the dark yellow has been worked in the last sequence, K 3 more R in dark yellow. Cast off in dark yellow.

Light Stripes (5 required): Using beige, cast on 40 sts and K 3 R.

R 4: K 1, K 2 together, K until 2 sts remain, K into front and back of next st, K1. **R 5:** P.

Repeat these 2 R until 23 R of beige have been worked. Continue in Color Sequence, working 20 R in each color. When the light yellow has been worked in the last sequence, K 3 more R in light yellow. Cast off in light yellow.

Finishing: Block strips wrong side up, then press with a warm iron over a damp cloth. Arrange the dark and light stripes alternately and sew together on the wrong side with backstitch. Press seams.

The diagonal stripes in each strip are produced by increasing at one side and decreasing at the other side of the same row.

Knitted patchwork geometry

FOR ALL

Size: 40 cm or 16" square.

Materials Required:

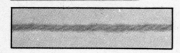

100 gm or 4 oz in main color (plus complementary Back color), 50 gm or 2 oz each of contrasting colors [50 gm = 200 m or 220 yds]. Knitting needles size 2 (Am) or 11 (Eng). Cushion pad 40 cm (16") square.

Basic Stitch: Stocking or stockinette stitch.

Tension: 29 sts and 40 R = 10 cm or 4".

Abbreviations: St(s) = stitch(es). R = row(s).

Design A (top left)

Colors: Main color: dark green. Contrasting colors: light green and turquoise.

Front: Make 4 rectangles in dark green and 2 in each of light green and turquoise. **Cast on 30 sts and work in stocking or stockinette stitch for 20 cm or 8". Cast off.

Back: Using dark green, cast on 116 sts and work in stocking stitch for 40 cm or 16". Cast off.

Finishing: Press work with a warm iron over a damp cloth. Arrange Front as shown in photograph and sew seams with backstitch on wrong side. Sew Back and Front edges together, leaving one end open. Insert cushion; sew closed**.

Design B (bottom left)

Colors: Main color: tur-quoise. Contrasting colors: dark green and orange.

Front: Work from ** to ** of Design A. Make 4 rectangles in dark green and 2 each in turquoise and orange. Work back in turquoise.

Design C (top center)

Colors: Main color: orange. Contrasting colors: light and dark green.

Front: Work in stocking or stockinette stitch.

Light green: Make 1 small square, casting on 24 sts and working for 8 cm or $3\frac{1}{8}$". Cast off. Make 2 large squares, casting on 48 sts and working for 16 cm or $6\frac{1}{4}$". Cast off.

Orange: Make 1 rectangle, casting on 48 sts and working for 8 cm or $3\frac{1}{8}$". Cast off. Make 1 rectangle, casting on 24 sts and working for 16 cm or $6\frac{1}{4}$". Cast off.

Dark green: Make 1 rectangle; cast on 48 sts and work for 24 cm or $9\frac{1}{2}$". Cast off. Make 1 rectangle, casting on 72 sts and working for 16 cm or $6\frac{1}{4}$".

Back: Work in orange as for Design A.

Finish as for Design A.

Design D (bottom center)

Colors: Main color: dark green. Contrasting colors: light green and turquoise.

Front: Work in stocking or stockinette stitch.

Dark green: Make 2 squares, casting on 30 sts and working for 10 cm or 4". Cast off.

Light green: Make 2 squares, casting on 60 sts and working for 20 cm or 8". Cast off.

Turquoise: Make 2 angled pieces, casting on 60 sts and working for 10 cm or 4"; end after a knit R. Cast off 30 sts at beginning of next R and continue straight for 10 cm or 4".

Back: Work in dark green as for Design A.

Finish as for Design A.

Design E (right)

Colors: Main color: turquoise. Contrasting colors: dark green and orange.

Front: Work in stocking or stockinette stitch.

Dark green. Make 1 square, casting on 30 sts and working for 10 cm or 4". Cast off. Make 1 angled piece, casting on 116 sts and working for 10 cm or 4"; end after a knit R. Cast off 86 sts at beginning of next R, then continue straight until piece measures 40 cm or 16" from beginning. Cast off.

Orange: Make 1 angled piece, casting on 88 sts and working for 10 cm or 4"; end after a knit R. Cast off 58 sts at beginning of next R, then continue straight until piece measures 30 cm or 12". Cast off.

Turquoise: Make 1 angled piece, casting on 60 sts and working for 10 cm or 4"; end after a knit R. Cast off 30 sts at beginning of next R then continue straight until piece measures 20 cm or 8". Cast off.

Back: Work in turquoise as for Design A.

Finish as for Design A.

Often, it is the small details such as sofa cushions which give character to a room. Angles, rectangles, and squares are knitted separately and sewn together to form these patchwork geometrics.

285

Made for me

Size: Directions are for 56 cm (22″) chest. Changes for 58, 60 cm (23″, 23¾″) chest are in brackets.

Materials Required:

150 (150:200) gm or 6 (6:8) oz navy blue, 50 gm or 2 oz each orange, green, red, and light blue [100 gm = 390 m or 425 yds]. Knitting needles and set of double-pointed needles size 2 (Am) or 11 (Eng). Elastic for skirt waist. Stitch holder.

Basic Pattern: See two-color knitting How-to. **R 1:** (right side): K in navy. **2nd and even-numbered R:** P in color of previous R. **R 3:** With orange, K 1, ∗K 1, K 1 into R below, K 1, slip 1 purlwise, yarn behind needle. Repeat from ∗ to last 4 sts, K 1, K 1 into R below, K 2. **R 5:** With red, K 1, ∗K 1, slip 1 purlwise, K 1, K 1 into R below. Repeat from ∗ to last 4 sts, K 1, slip 1 purlwise, K 2. **R 7:** With navy, repeat R 3. **R 9:** With navy, K. **R 11:** With green, repeat R 3. **R 13:** With light blue, repeat R 5. **R 15:** Navy, repeat R 3. **R 17:** With navy, K. **R 18:** With navy, P. R 3–18 form the repeat pattern.

Tension: 24 sts and 42 R = 10 cm or 4″.

Abbreviations: St(s) = stitch(es). R = row(s). K = knit. P = purl.

PULLOVER

Back: Using navy, cast on 65 (73:77) sts and work in K 1, P 1 rib for 5 (6:6) cm or 2″ (2½″:2½″). Change to Basic Pattern and work straight until piece is 16 (18.5:20) cm or 6¼″ (7¼″: 7¾″).

Shape Armholes: Cast off 2 sts at beginning of next 6 R, then decrease 1 st at each end of next 2 (3:3) R − 49 (55:59) sts. Work straight until piece is 28 (31:33) cm or 11″ (12¼″:13″), ending after a P R.

Shape Neck and Shoulders: Cast off center 19 (21:23) sts for neck and continue on sts at one side. At the beginning of every 2nd neck edge R, cast off 2 sts 2 times and decrease 1 st 1 time. *At the same time,* at the beginning of every 2nd armhole edge row, cast off 2 (3:3) sts once, 2 (2:3) sts once, 3 (3:3) sts once, 3 (4:4) sts once. Repeat for other side.

Front: Work to match Back to 23 (25:28) cm or 9″ 10″:11″); end after a P R.

Shape Neck: Cast off center 7 (9:9) sts and continue on sts at 1 side. At the beginning of every 2nd neck edge R, cast off 2 sts 2 times, then decrease 1 st on next 7 (7:8) R. Work straight until piece is 28 (31:33) cm or 11″ (12¼″:13″), then shape shoulder as for Back. Work other side to match.

Sleeves: Using navy, cast on 38 (40:44) sts and work 4 cm or 1½″ in K 1, P 1 rib. Change to stocking or stockinette stitch, increasing 1 st each end of every 12th (12th:14th) R 7 times − 52 (54:58) sts. Work straight until sleeve measures 26 (28:29) cm or 10¼″ (11″: 11½″) or length required.

Shape Shoulder: Cast off 2 sts at beginning of next 6 R, then decrease 1 st each end of next 10 (11:12) R. Cast off 2 sts at beginning of next 6 R. Cast off remaining 8 (8:10) sts.

Neck Border: Join shoulders. Using double-pointed needles and navy, pick up 94 (98:102) sts around neck edge on right side of piece and work in K 1, P 1 rib for 2.5 cm or 1″. Cast off.

SKIRT

Front and Back: Using navy, cast on 97 (105:109) sts and K 3 R. Work R 1–14 of Basic Pattern. Continue in navy in stocking or stockinette stitch for 3 R. **Next R:** K 30 (32:34), K 2 together, K 33 (37:37), slip 1, K 1, pass slip stitch over, K to end. Alternately in every 6th and 4th R, work this decreasing R, working 1 st less before and after decrease each time until 10 (11:13) decrease R have been worked. *At the same time,* when 12 R of stocking or stockinette st have been worked in navy, decrease 1 st each end of next and every 12th (11th:10th) R 4 (5:6) times. Work straight until piece is 17 (19:20) cm or 6¾″ (7½″:8″) or length required, then work 2 cm or ¾″ in rib. Cast off in rib.

Finishing: Press work on wrong side, omitting the ribbing. Pullover: Sew in sleeves, then sew up sleeve and side seams. Skirt: Sew up side seams. Make a herringbone stitch casing and thread elastic through.

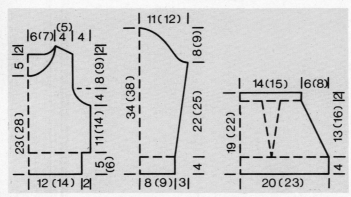

Measurements are given in centimeters; inch equivalents are in the directions.

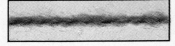

Like father, like son

SON

Size: Directions are for a 66 cm or 26″ chest. Changes for a 71 cm or 28″ chest are in brackets.

Materials Required:

300 (350) gm or 11 (13) oz dark brown, 50 gm or 2 oz light brown [100 gm = 240 m or 260 yds]. Knitting needles and a circular needle size 4 (Am) or 9 (Eng). 4 buttons.

Basic Pattern: R 1 (right side): K 1, P 2, *K 2, P 4, repeat from * to last 5 sts, K 2, P 2, K 1. **R 2:** K 3, *P 2, K 4, repeat from * to last 5 sts, P 2, K 3. These 2 R form the pattern.

Tension: 24 sts and 32 R = 10 cm or 4″.

Abbreviations: St(s) = stitch(es). R = row(s). K = knit. P = purl.

DIRECTIONS

Back: Using dark brown, cast on 80 (86) sts and work 8 cm or 3¼″ in K 1, P 1 rib. Change to Basic Pattern and continue straight to 29 (32) cm or 11½″ (12½″).

Shape Armholes: Cast off 3 sts at beginning of next 6 R. Continue straight on 62 (68) sts to 44 (48) cm or 17¼″ (18¾″).

Shape Shoulder and Neck: Cast off center 28 sts for the neck edge, then work separately on the 17 (20) sts at each side, shaping neck by casting off 2 sts 1 time and 1 st 1 time at beginning of neck edge R. *At the same time,* cast off 4 (5) sts on next armhole edge R and 5 (6) sts on next 2 armhole edge R.

Left Front: Using dark brown, cast on 38 (42) sts and work 8 cm or 3¼″ in K 1, P 1 rib. Change to Basic Pattern and work

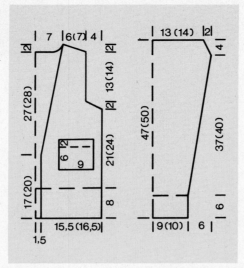

Half-pattern for the Son's cardigan. Measurements are in centimeters; inches are in the directions.

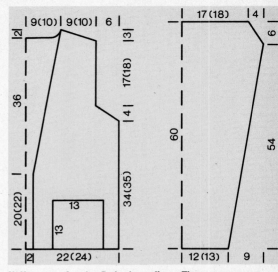

Half-pattern for the Father's cardigan. The measurements are given in centimeters; inch equivalents are in the directions.

straight to 17 (20) cm or 6½″ (7¾″). Shape Front by decreasing 1 st at front edge on next R and every 6th R 15 (16) times. *At the same time*, shape armhole and shoulder to match Back.

Right Front: Work to match Left Front, reversing shapings.

Sleeves: Using dark brown, cast on 44 (50) sts and work in K 1, P 1 rib for 6 cm or 2½″. Change to Basic Pattern and increase 1 st each end of every 8th (9th) R 14 (13) times. Continue straight to 43 (46) cm or 17″ (18″), then work 4 R in light brown, 4 R dark brown, and 4 R light brown. *At the same time*, decrease 1 st at beginning of next 12 R. Cast off remaining 60 (64) sts.

Pocket: Using dark brown, cast on 20 sts and work in Basic Pattern for 6 cm or 2½″ then change to K 1, P 1 rib and work 2 R light brown, 2 R dark brown, and 2 R light brown. Cast off in Rib Pattern.

Border: Join shoulders. Using circular needle and light brown, pick up 41 (49) sts along each straight front edge, 80 sts up shaped fronts and 46 sts along neck edge. Work 3 R light brown, 2 R dark brown, and 3 R light brown in K 1, P 1 rib. *At the same time,*

when working the 2 dark brown R, make buttonholes. Make 1st one 2.5 cm or 1″ from lower edge and 3 more at 3.5 (4.5) cm or 1¼″ (1¾″) intervals, by casting off 2 sts at these positions in 1st R and casting on 2 sts in next R. Cast off in rib.

Finishing: Press work. Sew in sleeves, then sew up sleeve and side seams. Sew pocket on left front about 10 cm or 4″ above ribbing. Sew on buttons.

FATHER

Size: Directions are for a 92 cm or 36″ chest. Changes for a 100 cm or 39½″ chest are in brackets.

Materials Required: Yarn: (see sample for Son's cardigan) 500 (550) gm or 18 (20) oz light brown. 50 gm or 2 oz dark brown. Knitting needles and a circular needle size 4 (Am) or 9 (Eng). 3 buttons.

Basic Pattern: R 1: K 3, *P 3, K 5, repeat from * to last 6 sts, P 3, K 3. R 2: K 1, P 2, *K 3, P 5, repeat from * to last 6 sts, K 3, P 2, K 1. Repeat these 2 R.

Tension and Abbreviations: See Son's cardigan.

DIRECTIONS

Back: Using light brown, cast on 113 (121) sts and work in Basic Pattern until

piece measures 34 (35) cm or 13½″ (13¾″).

Shape Armholes: Cast off 2 sts at beginning of next 12 R. Continue straight on 89 (97) sts to 55 (57) cm or 21½″ (22½″). At armhole edge, cast off 4 sts on next 2 R, 4 (5) sts 4 times, and 5 (5) sts 4 times. *At the same time,* when work measures 56 (58) cm or 22″ (22¾″) cast off center 35 (39) sts for neck. Working on each side separately, cast off 2 sts on next 2 neck edge R and decrease 1 st on the following neck edge R.

Left Front: Using light brown, cast on 52 (60) sts and work in Basic Pattern, but begin 1st R with K 6 instead of K 3 and end 2nd R K 3, P 5, K 1. Shape armhole and shoulder to match Back. *At the same time,* when work measures 20 (22) cm or 7¾″ (8½″), shape Front edge by decreasing 1 st on next and every 6th (5th) R, 17 (23) times.

Right Front: Work to match Left Front, reversing shaping and pattern (ie, 1st R ends K 6).

Sleeves: Using light brown, cast on 57 (65) sts and work in Basic Pattern, increasing 1 st each end of every 8th R 21 times – 99 (107) sts. Continue straight,

if necessary, to 54 cm or 21¼″. Now work 6 R each in dark brown and light brown. *At the same time,* decrease 1 st at beginning of next 18 R. Cast off remaining 81 (89) sts.

Pockets (2 required): Using light brown, cast on 31 sts and work in Basic Pattern, beginning and ending 1st R K 6 and 2nd R P 5 with edge st. Work for 11.5 cm or 4½″, then work 2 R each dark brown, light brown, and dark brown. Cast off.

Front Border: Join shoulders. Using circular needle and dark brown, pick up 50 (54) sts along each straight front edge, 94 sts along shaped Front edge, and 52 from Back neck. Work 2 R dark brown, 6 R light brown, and 2 R dark brown. *At the same time,* when working 3rd and 4th light brown R, make 3 buttonholes by casting off 4 sts in 1st R and casting on 4 sts in next R. Work 1st one 2 cm or ¾″ from lower edge of Left Front and 2 more at 6 (7) cm or 2½″ (2¾″) intervals along Border.

Finishing: Press. Sew in sleeves then sew up sleeve and side seams. Sew pockets in position shown in the diagram. Sew on buttons.

retty things to make

for her and her dolls

his is a perfect
astime for children.
is easy to knit
ng cords in bright
olors and fun
think up things
make with them.
Ve give some ideas
n the next page.

easy to shape the
ils into circles and squares
use as cushion covers.

Spool knitting
for children

Make yourself knitted cords in rainbow colors, then sew them into all kinds of different shapes. You can see how pretty they look. From these colored coils you can make small blankets, cushions, amusing animals, or clothes for your dolls. Just remember to sew backing fabric to larger items so that they keep their shape.

Knitting on a spool knitter

1 You will need a spool knitter, a fine knitting needle, and yarn. You can make a knitter with a thread spool and four nails.

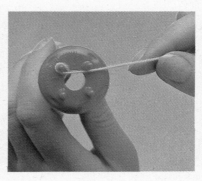

2 To cast on, put the yarn through the knitter from top to bottom and wind it around the post as shown.

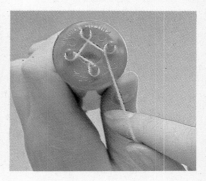

3 Continue to wind the yarn from right to left around each post. You are now ready to begin knitting the cord.

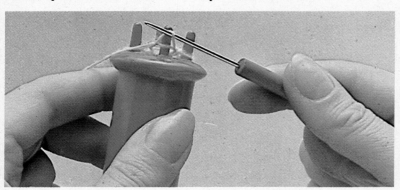

4 Bring the yarn past the first post so that it lies above the first loop. Put the needle into the loop and lift it over the yarn and the post. Turn the knitter to the next post and repeat. Continue to work in this manner until the cord is the required length.

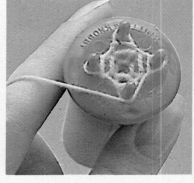

5 From time to time, pull the cord down into the knitter. When you have knitted 1 cm ($\frac{1}{2}$"), the stitches form a spider web.

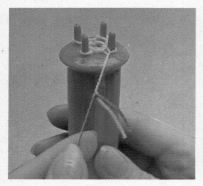

6 To join a new strand, tie the two pieces together and continue to knit. Stuff the ends into the center of the cord.

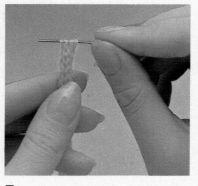

7 To end the cord, lift it from the knitter and thread the end of the yarn through the four loops. Pull the yarn tight.

8 Sew the coils together with overcasting on the wrong side, using yarn and a blunt-ended needle. Weave in the yarn ends.

Crafts

ese toy accessories and tiny mice
 all made from knitted coils of
rn in different lengths and colors.

nd a cord around a large cotton ball and sew
 coils together loosely. Sew on felt ears, bead
s, and yarn whiskers. Embroider the nose.

 a striped scarf, make several cords of different
ors. Knot the ends and sew the cords together
h matching yarn.

Take two long cords and begin in the middle with a knot. From there, wind and stitch the two cords in parallel coils around the doll's head until the cap is large enough. Turn in the two ends at the back of the cap and secure them on the wrong side.

ld three cords side by side and form them into
spiral. Sew them in place. Make a loop at the
. Make the back from a scrap of cotton fabric.

Start winding from the feet of the baby doll, and stitching the coils together invisibly. For the head-piece, coil the cords in a circle.

Make a braid. Take it back over right shoulder, then around tummy. Make a loop at back and bring end over left shoulder to front. Stitch in place.

Create a coat of many colors

This casual cardigan is a perfect jacket to wear with shirts and colorful jerseys. The interlocking color pattern and the three-dimensional texture are made by working double crochets over the stitches of the previous row.

FOR BOTH

Size: Directions are for 134 cm (52¾") height and 68 cm (26¾") chest. Changes for 146 cm (57½") height, 73 cm (28¾") chest are in brackets.

Materials Required:

Colors and amounts are given in individual directions [50 gm = 140 m or 153 yds]. Crochet hook size 7. 5 buttons.

Sleeve Pattern: Repeat rows 11 and 12 of Stitch Pattern for boy's cardigan. In first pattern row, work rel dc into sc in last odd row.

Border Stitch: Sc, chain 1 to turn.

Tension: 18 sts and 22 R = 10 cm or 4".

Abbreviations: St(s) = stitch(es). R = row(s). Sc = single crochet. Rel dc = relief double crochet.

BOY'S CARDIGAN

Yarn Required: 200 (250) gm or 7 (9) oz olive green, 100 gm or 4 oz each of white, dark red, and yellow.

Stitch Pattern: Row 1: (right side) sc chain 1 to turn. Row 2 and all even rows: Sc beginning in 2nd st, ending in turning chain. Row 3: Beginning in 2nd st, 2 (1:2) sc, *1 rel dc on right side into next st in 1st R, 2 sc, repeat from *, chain 1, turn. Row 5: *2 sc, 1 rel dc around rel dc in last odd row, 2 sc, repeat from *, chain 1, turn. Rows 7 and 9: Repeat R 5. Row 11: *5 sc, 1 rel dc around rel dc of last odd R, repeat from *, chain 1, turn. Rows

13, 15, 17: Repeat R 11. Repeat rows 2–18.

Color Sequence: *2 R olive green, 2 R white, 2 R red, 2 R yellow, repeat from *.

GIRL'S CARDIGAN

Yarn Required: 200 (250) gm or 7 (9) oz yellow, 100 gm or 4 oz each of white and olive green.

Stitch Pattern: Work R 1–6 as for boy's cardigan, then repeat R 5 and 6 to end of piece.

Color Sequence: *2 R white, 2 R yellow, 2 R olive green, repeat from *.

DIRECTIONS

Back: Chain 56 (59) sts in yellow for girl or green for boy. Sc in 2nd chain from hook and in each chain across, chain 1, turn. Work straight in Border Stitch. At 7 cm or 2¾", add 10 sts evenly distributed across row — 65 (68) sts. Continue in Stitch Pattern and Color Sequence.

Shape Armhole: At 31 (33) cm or 12¼" (13"), at each side in every row, decrease by slip-stitching the sts at the beginning of the R, and leaving them unworked at the end of the R. Decrease 2 sts 2 times, 1 st 2 times, then in every 2nd R, 1 st 3 times — 47 (50) sts. Continue to work straight in the established pattern.

Shape Shoulder: At 45 (48) cm or 17¾" (19"), decrease 2 sts 1 time and 3 sts 3 times (3 sts 3 times and 4 sts 1 time). *At the same time,* for the neck edge, leave the center 17 (16) sts unworked. At either side of these sts, in every R, decrease 2 sts 1 time and 1 st 2 times.

The interlocking effect of the relief stitch makes the color pattern of the boy's cardigan appear more intricate than it is.

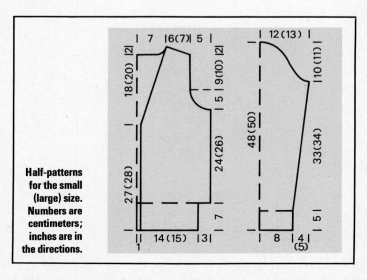

Half-patterns for the small (large) size. Numbers are centimeters; inches are in the directions.

Right Front: Chain 28 (31) in yellow or green and work straight in Border Stitch. At 7 cm or 2¾", add 5 sts evenly distributed across row — 32 (35) sts. Continue in Stitch Pattern and Color Sequence, shaping side, armhole, and shoulder as for Back. *At the same time,* at 27 (28) cm or 10⅝" (11"), decrease 1 st every 4th R 12 (13) times at front edge.

Left Front: Work to match Right Front, reversing the shapings.

Sleeves: Chain 30 in yellow or green and work straight in Border Stitch. At 5 cm or 2", begin Color Sequence and Stitch Pattern, working 2 sc instead of 5 sc at the beginning of the pattern rows. Increase 1 st at each side of every 10th R 7 times (every 8th R 9 times) — 43 (47) sts.

Shape Armhole: At 38 (39) cm or 15" (15⅜"), at each side of every R, decrease 2 sts 1 time and 1 st 4 (5) times, 1 st in every 2nd R 7 times, 1 st in every R 2 (3) times, and 2 sts 1 time.

Finishing: Join all seams. Work 1.5 cm or ⅝" of sc in yellow or green around Front and Neck edges, working 45 (48) sts on straight Front edges, 38 (40) sts on slanted edges, and 27 sts across Back. At 1.5 cm or ⅝", work buttonholes on girl's Right Front and boy's Left Front. Make the 1st buttonhole 3 sts from the lower edge by chaining 2, skipping 2 sts, and working sc in next st. Make buttonholes 9 (10) sts apart. Continue to work in sc until the edging is 3 cm or 1¼". Sew on buttons.

Relief double crochet

Relief double crochet with single crochet

1 Pass the hook under the yarn and insert the hook into the front of the next single crochet stitch two rows below the row you are working.

2 Draw the yarn through the stitch. Pass the hook under the yarn and work a double crochet on the front of the piece in the usual way.

3 One relief double crochet has been made. Work the specified number of single crochets, then make another relief double crochet. Continue in this way.

4 In all other pattern rows, make the relief double crochet into the relief stitch below it. The rows in between are worked in single crochet.

Relief double crochet with double crochet

1 Pass the hook under the yarn and insert the hook behind the middle of the next double crochet in the row below the row you are working.

2 Draw the yarn through the stitch. Pass the hook under the yarn and work a double crochet on the front of the piece in the usual way.

3 Work the specified number of double crochets between the relief stitches. Work the rows between the double crochet pattern rows in single crochet.

4 Work the relief double crochets around previous relief stitches, or for a staggered pattern, work around double crochets between relief stitches.

Sweater duo-
made for each other

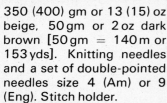
PULLOVER

Size: Directions are for 88 cm (34½") bust. Changes for 96 cm (37½") bust are in brackets.

Materials Required:

350 (400) gm or 13 (15) oz beige, 50 gm or 2 oz dark brown [50 gm = 140 m or 153 yds]. Knitting needles and a set of double-pointed needles size 4 (Am) or 9 (Eng). Stitch holder.

Basic Stitch: Reverse stocking or stockinette stitch, with P as right side.

Tension: 23 sts and 34 R = 10 cm or 4".

Abbreviations: St(s) = stitch(es). R = row(s). K = knit. P = purl.

DIRECTIONS

Back: Using dark brown, cast on 110 (120) sts and work 3 cm or 1¼" in K 1, P 1 rib. Continue with beige yarn in Basic Stitch. Work until piece measures 8 cm or 3¼", then decrease 1 st at each end of next and every 7th R 6 times 96 (106) sts. Work straight until Back measures 27 cm or 10½", then increase 1 st at each end of every 10th R 5 times. Work straight until piece measures 44 (43) cm or 17¼" (17"). Shape Armholes: Cast off 3 sts at beginning of next 2 R, 2 sts at beginning of next 4 R, then decrease 1 st at each end of next 7 R — 78 (88) sts. Work straight until piece is 63 cm or 24¾". Shape Neck and Shoulders: Cast off the center 34 sts and work on sts at one side. At neck edge, cast

Choose a color and another for contrast, then knit the pullover with the purl side as the right side. Add ribbed borde

off 2 sts in the next R and decrease 1 st on the 2nd R. *At the same time*, at the shoulder edge, cast off 6 (8) sts at the beginning of every 2nd R 2 times, 7 (8) sts 1 time. Work other side to match.

Front: Work as for Back until Front measures 56 cm or 22".

Shape Neck: Cast off center 12 sts and work on sts at one side. Cast off 2 sts at neck edge every 2nd R 3 times, then decrease 1 st on next 8 neck edge R. Shape shoulder to match Back at 63 cm or 24¾". Work other side to match.

Sleeves: Using dark brown, cast on 48 (58) sts and work 6 cm or 2½" in K 1, P 1 rib. Continue in Basic Stitch with beige yarn. Increase 1 st each end of every 8th R 15 times — 78 (88) sts. Work straight until sleeve is 45 cm or 17¾".

Shape Top: Cast off 3 sts at beginning of next 2 R,

2 sts in next 6 (10) R, decrease 1 st each end of next 14 (10) R, cast off 2 sts at beginning of next 6 (10) R and 4 sts on next 2 R. Cast off.

Neck Border: Join shoulders. Using double-pointed needles and brown, work 3 cm or 1¼" in K 1, P 1 rib on 120 sts at neck edge. Cast off in rib.

Finishing: Press lightly. Sew in sleeves. Sew seams.

VEST

Materials Required: Yarn: (see sample for pullover) 200 gm or 8 oz beige, 100 gm or 4 oz each dark brown and rust. Crochet hook size F. 6 buttons.

Basic Pattern: See chart.

Tension: 20 sts and 10 R = 10 cm or 4".

Abbreviations: St(s) = stitch(es). R = row(s). Ch = chain. Sc = single crochet. Dc = double crochet.

DIRECTIONS

Back: Using dark brown, ch 102 (112) and work 1 sc into 3rd ch from hook, and in each ch across — 101 (111) sc. Ch 1 to turn and work 5 more R in sc. Change to Basic Pattern and work across 10 (11) pattern repeats, working 1 edge st (indicated by the double line) at beginning of right side R and end of wrong side R. Work straight until piece measures 7 cm or 2¾", then decrease 1 dc each end of next and every 2nd R until 83 (93) dc remain. Work straight to 27 cm or 10½", then increase 1 dc each end of next and every 4th R until there are 93 (103) dc. Work until Back measures 46 (45) cm or 18¼" (17¾").

Shape Armholes: Decrease at beginning of R by slip-stitching along and at end by turning and leaving last sts unworked. Decrease 6 (7) dc each end of next R, 2 dc each end of next 3 R,

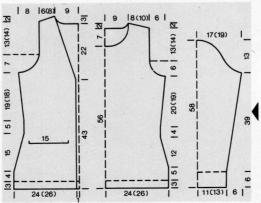

The vest can be worn on its own with shirts or blouses.

◄ Half-pattern for small (large) size. Numbers are centimeters; inches are given in the directions.

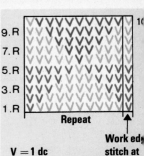

| 9. R |
| 7. R |
| 5. R |
| 3. R |
| 1. R |

Repeat

V = 1 dc
10 sts and
10 R =
1 repeat.

Work edge stitch at beginning or end of each row

302

1 dc each end of next
[?] — 61 (69) dc. Work
[r]ight until Back is 65 cm
[2]5½".

[Shap]e Neck and Shoulders:
[Lea]ve center 25 dc un-
[wor]ked, and work on sts
[of] one side. Decrease in
[ever]y R at neck edge 2 dc
[3 ti]mes and 1 dc 1 time.
[At t]he same time, at 66 cm
[or 2]6", decrease at armhole
[edg]e, 6 (8) dc in the 1st R
[and] 7 (9) dc in the 2nd R.

[Poc]ket Linings (2 re-
[quir]ed): Using beige, ch 32.
[Wor]k 1 dc into 4th ch from
[hoo]k and in each ch across.
[ch] 3 to turn and work in dc
[for] 15 cm or 6". Set pocket
[linin]gs aside.

[Righ]t Front: Using dark
[brow]n, ch 47 (52) and work
[1 R] of sc as for Back — 46
[(52)] sc. Change to Basic
[Patt]ern and work across 4½
[?] pattern repeats until
[piec]e measures 7 cm or
[3", t]hen shape outer edge
[as fo]r Back until 3 complete
[patt]ern repeats (30 R)
[hav]e been worked.

[Next] row (Front edge): Work
[to ?], leave next 30 dc and
[wor]k over 30 dc of one
[poc]ket lining, work to end.
[Shap]e side, armhole, and
[shou]lder as for Back. At the
[sam]e time, when piece
[mea]sures 43 cm or 17",
[decr]ease 1 dc at beginning
[of n]ext R, then every 2nd
[R 8] times.

[Left] Front: Work to match
[Righ]t Front, reversing
[shap]ings and Basic Pattern.

[Armh]ole Borders: Using
[dark] brown, ch 92 (96)
[and] work in sc for 4 R.

[Fron]t Border: Using dark
[brow]n, ch 308 and work in
[sc fo]r 2 R. In next R work
[8 bu]ttonholes — one 2 cm
[or ¾]" from lower edge, and
[8 mo]re 6 cm or 2¼" apart.
[For] each buttonhole, skip
[4 sc,] ch 4, and sc to next
[posi]tion. Work 2 sc R.

[Fini]shing: Press pieces.
[Sew] seams. Sew on bor-
[ders.] Sew on buttons. Sew
[the] pocket linings in place
[secu]rely along the side and
[botto]m edges.

Changing colors

Changing at the end of the row

1 At the end of the row, draw the new color through the last two loops of the last stitch of the row.

2 The turning chain is worked in the new color. Carry the unused color behind the work, but do not pull the yarn too tight.

3 Work the new row in the new color or follow the color pattern. See the directions at right for changing in the middle of a row.

Changing in the middle of a row

1 Draw the new color through the last two loops of the last stitch in the old color and continue in the new color.

2 When making only one stitch in the new color, work the last two loops of the stitch in the next color as before.

3 Using the method in step 2, you can make a single stitch in a different color. Carry the unused color loosely behind.

The zigzag pattern is double crochet and all of the borders are knitted on.

A knit and crochet combination

Size: Directions are for 96 cm or 37½" chest. Changes for 100 cm or 40" chest are in brackets.

Materials Required:

200 (250) gm or 8 (9) oz beige, 50 gm or 2 oz each of black and brown. Crochet hook size D. Knitting needles and a circular needle size 2.

Basic Stitch: Double crochet. Every R begins with 3 ch as 1st dc. Work from chart for 1st–6th R, repeating 1st–16th sts and alternating the color bands after each beige stripe.

Note: Follow chart from right to left for odd rows and left to right for even rows.

Border Pattern: Work in K 2, P 2 rib.

Tension: 22 sts and 12 R

Adding crochet onto knitting and knitting onto crochet

Adding crochet onto knitting

1 Insert the crochet hook into the next stitch on the knitting needle.

2 Pass hook under yarn and draw the loop through. Slip the stitch off the knitting needle.

3 Finish the stitch. Any crochet stitch can be worked onto a knitted stitch.

Adding knitting onto crochet

1 Insert the knitting needle into the top of the crochet stitches from front to back.

2 Pass the yarn over the needle from right to left and draw the yarn through the stitch.

3 Work the picked-up stitches in the stitch pattern given in the directions.

Crochet

A wavy pattern worked in double crochet and knitted ribbed borders are combined for an interesting texture blend.

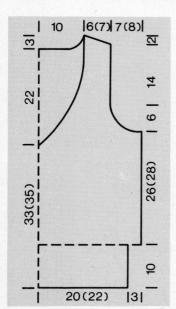

The measurements are in centimeters; inch equivalents are in the directions.

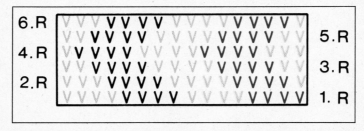

Color pattern: Rows 1–6 and stitches 1–16 are one whole repeat of the pattern.

= 10 cm or 4″.

Abbreviations: St(s) = stitch(es). R = row(s). Ch = chain. Dc = double crochet. Sc = single crochet. K = knit. P = purl.

DIRECTIONS

Back: Using knitting needles, cast on 112 (120) sts and work in Border Pattern for 10 cm or 4″.

Continue in dc. Following diagram, work 1 dc into each st on the left needle, repeating from 1st–16th sts 7 times (1st–16th sts 7 times, then 1st–8th sts 1 time). Continue straight until piece measures 36 (38) cm or 14¼″ (15″).

Shape Armholes: Decrease by slip-stitching at beginning of R; at end, turn and leave required number of dc unworked. At each end of every R, decrease 5 (7) dc 1 time, 2 dc 5 times, and 1 dc 3 times. Work straight on 76 (80) dc until piece measures 55 (57) cm or 21½″ (22½″).

Shape Neck and Shoulders: Leave center 32 dc unworked and work on each side separately, decreasing 2 dc at neck edge on next 2 R. Decrease 2 dc on following 2 neck edge R and *at the same time,* on next 3 armhole edge R decrease 4 (5) dc 1 time, 5 (5) dc 1 time, and 5 (6) dc 1 time. Fasten off.

Front: Work as for Back to 33 (35) cm or 13″ (13¾″).

Shape Neck: Divide the piece in center and work on 56 (60) dc each side separately. Shape armhole and shoulders to correspond with Back. *At the same time,* at neck edge, decrease 2 sts on next R, 1 st on next 8 R, and 1 st every 2nd R 4 times.

Neckband: Sew shoulders. Using crochet hook and beige, work 156 (160) sc around neck edge. Change to circular needle. Pick up and K 1 st into each sc, then work in Border Pattern, knitting center 2 sts and decreasing 1 st each side of these every alternate Rnd until neckband measures 4 cm or 1½″. Cast off in rib.

Armbands: Join side seams. Using crochet hook and beige, work 104 (108) sc around armhole. Change to circular needle. Pick up and K 1 st into each sc, then work in K 2, P 2 rib for 2 cm or ¾″. Cast off in rib pattern.

Finishing: Press work.

Soft style, soft colors

...ck your hair up under ...e soft folds of this beret ... a carefree approach to ...mp and windy weather.

...aterials Required:

...gm or 2 oz each green, ...k, medium blue, pale ...e, and brown. Crochet ...ok size D.

...sic Stitch: Rounds of ...uble crochet closed ...th a slip stitch and with ...ain-3 to begin each ...und.

...lor Sequence: 2 rounds ...ch of pale blue, brown, ...een, pink, medium blue, ...peat. Join new color in ...st chain at beginning of ...e round.

...nsion: 24 sts and 14 ...ds = 10 cm or 4".

...breviations: St(s) = ...tch(es). Rnd(s) = round(s). ... = row(s). Sc = single ...ochet. Dc = double ...ochet.

...RECTIONS
...ain 6. Slip stitch in 1st ...ain to form a ring, chain ... **Rnd 1:** 11 dc into ring.

The beret with fall in graceful folds around your face for a chic and flattering fashion.

Crochet the stripes in rounds of double crochet worked in bands of fashion-keyed colors.

Rnd 2: Dc, working 2 dc into every 3rd dc of the previous rnd — 24 sts. **Rnd 3:** Dc, working 2 dc into every 2nd dc. **Rnd 4:** Dc, working 2 dc into every 3rd st — 48 sts. **Rnd 5:** Dc, working 2 dc into every 4th st — 60 sts. **Rnd 6:** Dc, working 2 dc into every 5th st — 72 sts. **Rnd 7:** Dc, working 2 dc into every 6th st — 84 sts. Continue in this way, increasing in each st which corresponds with number of previous row worked. In other words, in rnd 8, increase in every 7th st. At the end of rnd 18 there will be 216 sts.

Rnd 19: Work every 17th and 18th dc together — 204 sts. **Rnd 20:** Work every 16th and 17th sts together — 192 sts. Continue in this way, working together the 15th and 16th sts in rnd 21, the 14th and 15th sts in rnd 22, and so on. At the end of rnd 28 there will be 96 sts. For the edge, work 10 rnds of sc in Color Sequence.

A matching scarf

When you have finished your beret, you will have yarn left over, so make a scarf to match.

For a 15 cm (6") wide scarf, chain 39 sts. For a 20 cm (8") wide scarf, chain 51. Work straight in R of dc, with a chain-3 for turning. Work 4 R in each color rather than 2 R, to avoid changing color so often. Always begin the new color in the 1st chain of the turning chain.

For fringe, cut strands about 30 cm (12") long. Knot several strands in a variety of colors into each st along the ends.

Confetti fashions for little girls... and big ones too!

Crocheted vest is designed for little girls, with a matching one for mother or big sister.

CHILD'S VEST

Size: Directions are for a 62 cm (24¼") chest. Changes for the 66 cm (26") chest are in brackets.

Materials Required:

100 gm or 4 oz red, 50 gm or 2 oz each of blue, dark green, white, and pink [50 gm = 130 m or 140 yds]. Crochet hooks sizes E and F.

Basic Pattern: Into 4th st from hook work 1 sc, 1 ch, 1 dc (known as 1 group), *skip 1 ch, 1 group into next ch. Repeat from * to last ch, 1 half dc into ch, ch 2, turn.

Each Pattern R: Work 1 group into each ch loop, but with half dc in last ch loop, turn with ch 2.

Pattern Diagram: R 1–8, and sts 1–8 form the pattern, but note that when working R 1 and R 2 work from right to left and for R 3 and R 4, work from left to right. Follow colors for pattern, alternating white and pink where necessary.

Tension: 24 sts and 14 R = 10 cm or 4".

Abbreviations: St(s) = stitch(es). R = row(s). Ch = chain. Sc = single crochet. Dc = double crochet.

DIRECTIONS

Work Front and Back in one

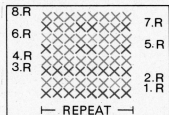

Pattern diagram: Each X = 1 group in the correct color sequence.

◀ Half-pattern for the small (large) sizes. Numbers are centimeters; inches are given in the directions.

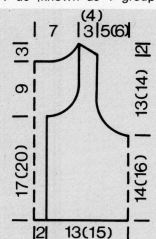

piece to armholes. Using red and F hook ch 88 (104), join on blue and ch 4. Work the Basic Pattern, following Pattern Diagram — 44 (52) patterns and 5½ (6½) repeats. Work straight until piece measures 14 (16) cm or 5½" (6¼"), ending after a P R.

Right Front: Work across 10 (12) groups; turn. Shape armhole by slip-stitching over 2 groups on next R and over 1 group every 2nd R 2 (3) times — 6 (7) groups remain. *At the same time,* when piece measures 17 (20) cm or 6½" (7¾"), shape neck by slip-stitching over 2 groups in next R, then 1 group every 2nd R 2 times. Continue straight on the 2 (3) groups until piece measures 27 (30) cm or 10½" (11¾"). Shape shoulder by decreasing 1 group at beginning of next 2 (3) right side R.

Left Front: Work last 10 (12) groups to match Right Front, reversing shapings.

Back: Go back to remaining 24 (28) groups and decrease 2 groups each end of next R and 1 group each end of every 2nd R 2 (3) times. Continue straight on the 16 (18) groups until piece measures 26 (29) cm or 10¼" (11½"). Leave center 6 groups and work on each side separately, decreasing 1 group at neck edge on next 3 R. *At the same time,* when piece measures same as Front to shoulder, decrease 1 group on each end of next 2 (3) R.

Armhole and Front Borders: Join shoulders. Using the F hook and red, work 1 R of dc around each armhole. Using the E hook, work border by alternating 4 groups each of green and blue. Work 15 (18) groups along each Front edge and 38 groups around shaped Front and Back neck. Now work 2 more R in pattern, but at corner of last row work 2 groups into each corner group.

Finishing: Press lightly.

WOMAN'S VEST

Size: Directions are for the 80 cm (31½″). Changes for the 88 cm (34½″) are in brackets.

Materials Required: Yarn (see sample for Child's Vest). 100 (150) gm or 4 (6) oz of red and 50 gm or 2 oz each of blue, dark

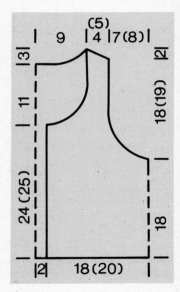

Half-pattern for the small (large) sizes. Numbers are centimeters; inches are given in the directions.

The confetti vest looks good on big girls, too! ▶

en, white, and pink.
ochet hooks sizes E and

sic Pattern, Pattern
agram, Tension, and
breviations: See Child's
st.

RECTIONS

rk Front and Back in one
ce to armholes. Using
F hook and red, ch 120
36); join on blue and ch
Work in Basic Pattern,
owing Pattern Diagram—
(68) groups and $7\frac{1}{2}$ ($8\frac{1}{2}$)
eats. Work straight until
ce measures 18 cm or
, ending after a wrong
e R.

ght Front: Work across
(16) groups; turn.
crease 2 groups at next
mhole edge, 1 group on
xt 2 armhole edge R,
en 1 group every 2nd R 1
times — 9 (10) groups
nain. Continue straight
24 (25) cm or $9\frac{1}{2}$" ($9\frac{3}{4}$")
ding at Front edge.

ape Neck: At Front edge,
crease 2 groups once, 1
up 2 times, and 1 group
ery 2nd R 2 times. Work
aight on 3 (4) groups to
(37) cm or $14\frac{1}{4}$" ($14\frac{1}{2}$").
ape shoulder by decreas-
at armhole edge 1
up 2 times and 1 (2)
up(s) 1 time.

ft Front: Work to match
ght Front, reversing
apings.

ck: Work on remaining
, decreasing at each end
match Front armholes.
rk straight on 22 (24)
ups to 35 (36) cm or
$\frac{1}{4}$" ($14\frac{1}{4}$"). Leave center
groups unworked and
rk on each side sepa-
ely, decreasing 1 group
next 4 neck edge R.
en work measures 36
7) cm or $14\frac{1}{4}$" ($14\frac{1}{2}$"),
ape shoulder to match
onts.

**mhole and Front
orders:** Work as for
ild's Vest, but also work
(21) groups along Front
ges and 46 groups
ound neck.
nishing: See Child's Vest.

Crocheted color group

How-to

1 Finish each group in its own color, then draw the new color through the next stitch.

2 Make a single crochet by drawing new color through both loops; chain 1. Yarn lies behind work.

3 When making double crochets, place other colors behind work; secure when making the first loop.

4 This is the reverse side as seen when working a return row and making two-color single crochet.

5 The other color lies loose in front of the single crochet. Chain one to continue group.

6 To work double crochet on reverse side, lay loose color in front; secure it with first loop.

Follow the photograph from top to bottom to work the pretty mesh pattern of diamonds and zigzags.

Cotton and washable

The charm of lace

Soft light through a lacy curtain creates a cozy, feminine atmosphere in a room. The pattern is worked in filet mesh crochet.

Size: 150 cm (59″) wide x 132 cm (52″) long.

Materials Required:

550 gm or 20 oz ecru [50 gm = 300 m or 330 yds]. Crochet hook size B.

Stitch Pattern: For spaces: Ch 2, 1 tr into tr in previous R. For blocks: 3 tr into next 3 sts.

Tension: 35 sts and 9½ R = 10 cm or 4″.

Abbreviations: St(s) = stitch(es). R = row(s). Ch = chain. Tr = treble. Dc = double crochet. Sc = single crochet.

DIRECTIONS

Work curtain from top to bottom. Chain 523. R 1: 1 tr into 5th chain from hook, 1 tr into each of next 2 ch, ch 2, skip 2 ch, 1 tr into each of next 4 ch, *ch 2, skip 2 ch, 1 tr into next ch, repeat from * to last 12 ch, then ch 2, skip 2 ch, 1 tr into each of next 4 ch, ch 2, skip 2 ch, 1 tr into each of last 4 ch, ch 4 to turn. R 2: Skip 1st st, 3 tr, ch 2, skip 2 sts, 4 tr, *(ch 2, skip 2 sts, 1 tr) 11 times, 3 tr, repeat from * 13 times, ch 2, skip 2 sts, 4 tr. R 3: 4 tr, ch 2, skip 2 sts, 4 tr, (ch 2, skip 2 sts, 1 tr) 10 times, *3 tr, ch 2, skip 2 sts, 4 tr, (ch 2, skip 2 sts, 1 tr) 9 times, repeat from * ending ch 2, skip 2 sts, 4 tr, ch 2, skip 2 sts, 4 tr.

Working 4 tr, ch 2, skip 2 sts, 4 tr at each end for edging, work curtain pattern. Follow the picture at left from top to bottom and the filet mesh How-to. After the 115th R, decrease 3 sts at each end of the next 3 R. At the 119th R, begin working the pointed border (see How-to). On beginning ch R, work a R of dc, working 1 dc into tr, and 2 dc into spaces. Work 1 R of dc, then 2 R sc. Finally, work slip stitch around pointed edges.

Finishing: Wet curtain in a starch solution. Pin out and leave to dry.

Working designs in filet mesh

Filet crochet

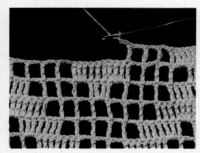

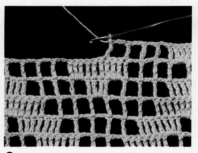

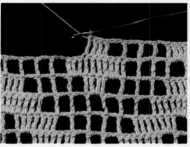

1 Spaces: Chain the required number of stitches, skip the same number of stitches, then work into the next stitch.

2 Blocks: Work stitches into each stitch of the block or around each chain of the spaces in the previous row.

3 Design: Work spaces and blocks according to the pattern. On a graph pattern, each square indicates a space or block.

Pointed border

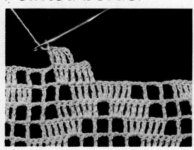

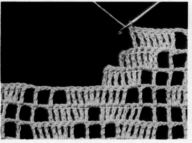

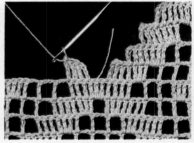

1 Work each point separately and in a stepped design. At the beginning of the row, slip-stitch stitches to be decreased.

2 At the end of the row, leave the stitches to be decreased unworked, chain 1, then slip-stitch to decrease for next row.

3 To begin the next point, skip the required number of blocks or spaces at the piece edge, join yarn, and work the point design.

Edging with slip stitch

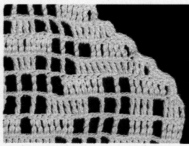

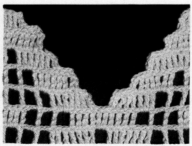

1 Begin to work the edging at one side of the curtain, starting with the three decreased rows just before the border points.

2 Work the edging by slip-stitching across all of the stitches of the stepped border. This creates a finished edge.

Testing the tension

Because of the stretchy nature of the fabric created by filet mesh, it is advisable to make a test swatch of at least 20 cm (8″) square rather than the standard 12 cm (5″). Pin out the piece and measure the center 10 cm (4″) to obtain an accurate measure of your stitch tension. When measuring the overall size of the piece, be careful not to stretch it out of shape.

Dressed in my Sunday best

Size: Directions are for 52 cm (20½″) chest. Changes for 56 cm (22″) chest are in brackets.

Materials Required:

200 (250) gm or 8 (9) oz red [50 gm = 149 m or 162 yds]. Crochet hook F.

Basic Pattern 1: R 1: Into 3rd st from hook, make 1 group of 1 sc, 2 dc, *skip 2 ch, 1 group into next ch. Repeat from * to end, 1 sc in last ch. R 2: Turn with 2 ch, then 1 group into center st of each group of previous R, ending 1 sc into turning ch. Repeat R 2.

Basic Pattern 2: Note: When working 1 ch to create a space, skip next st below. R 1: 3 ch, 2 dc, *1 ch, 1 dc, 1 ch, 1 dc, 1 ch, 3 dc. Repeat from * to end. R 2: 3 ch, *1 ch, 3 dc (working 1 dc on dc, 1 dc into space, 1 dc on dc). Repeat from * ending 1 ch, 1 dc. R 3: 3 ch, *1 ch, 1 dc, 1 ch, 3 dc, 1 ch, 1 dc, repeat from *, ending 1 ch, 1 dc. R 4: Repeat R 2. Repeat R 1–4.

Tension 1: 20 sts and 13 R = 10 cm or 4″.

Tension 2: 20 sts and 9 R = 10 cm or 4″.

Abbreviations: St(s) = stitch(es). R = row(s). Rnd(s) = round(s). Ch = chain. Sc = single crochet. Dc = double crochet. Gr = group.

DIRECTIONS

Skirt (6 panels required): Make 20 ch and work in Basic Pattern 1. Increase 1 st each end of every 3rd R and work increased sts in sc until there are 3 sc, then work 1 gr in 1 sc, skip 2 sc − 8 (9) times − 36 (38) sts. Continue to 18 (20) cm or 7″ (7¾″). Fasten off. Join panels together.

Top: Go back to beginning ch of skirt and with 3 ch as 1st dc, work *1 dc, 1 ch, skip 1 ch. Repeat from * all round; join with slip stitch. Rnd 2: Work 17 (19) dc evenly across 4 panels and 18 dc across each of last 2 panels − 104 (112) dc. Continue in Basic Pattern 2 in rnds, working from * of each rnd to 10 (11) cm or 4″ (4¼″).

Back: Work across only 52 (56) dc for Back and decrease 4 sts each end of next R, 2 sts each end of next R, and 1 st each end of next 2 R − 36 (40) dc. Work straight to 21 (23) cm or 8¼″ (9″). Leave center 12 dc unworked and decrease 2 sts each side of neck 3 times. *At the same time*, at 23 (25) cm or 9″ (9¾″), decrease 3 (4) sts twice at shoulder edge.

Front: Work on remaining 52 (56) sts to match Back, but at 14 (16) cm or 5½″ (6¼″), leave center 8 sts unworked. On each side, decrease 2 sts 2 times, 1 st 2 times, then in every 2nd R, 1 st 2 times.

Finishing: Work 1 rnd of sc around each armhole. Press.

◄ The dress is pretty with brightly patterned shirts and blouses.

Half-pattern ► for small (large) sizes. Measurements are in centimeters.

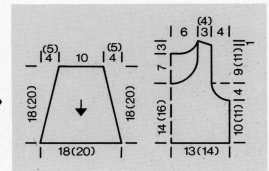

Skirt fashions with a flair

Smart stripes in pure handwoven silk.

The pattern for our lovely skirts is given in sizes C and E. Three other sizes can be adapted. The pleats are particularly distinctive as they are top-stitched to a point just below the hips and the fullness is then released for a flattering effect. If you are rather wide in the hips, avoid buying a fabric with horizontal stripes. They will emphasize rather than disguise your measurements. Also, matching up the stripes makes the job more difficult when you are learning to make pleats.

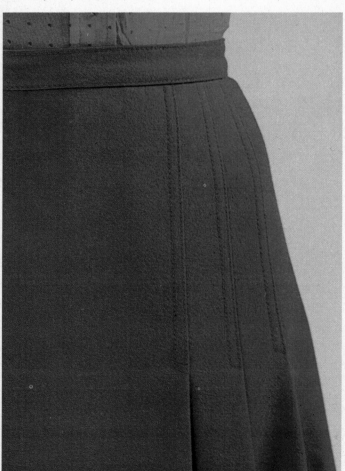

The three pleats on each side of the center front and back are top-stitched twice.

A useful skirt for everyday wear with blouses and sweaters.

The length of the pleats will make you look tall, slim, and elegant. The depth of the pleats also allows for maximum movement and they will swing gracefully as you move.

The pattern can be made in a longer style for evening and more formal wear. Make it in Shantung silk and natural raw silk – lovely to wear and beautiful to look at.

Making knife or side pleats

Knife or side pleats are made with the folds turned in one direction.

There are three important lines on knife or side pleats. First, there is the outside pleat fold line. This is the line on which the pleat is folded, pressed, and sometimes stitched on the right side. Then there is the pleat placement line. This is the line along which the pressed fold lies. Finally, there is the hidden pleat fold line. This is the fold line on the underside of the fabric.

Pleats tend to be narrower at the top to contour the waist and the hips. This shaping has the advantage of making the pleat less bulky. Accuracy is important! When making pleats, make sure that all the pleat lines are marked accurately on the fabric.

Transfer all contour lines and markings to the wrong side of the fabric, tracing them with dressmaker's tracing paper and a tracing wheel. But take care! First test the color on a fabric scrap. If the color shows through, mark the lines with tailor's tacks instead.

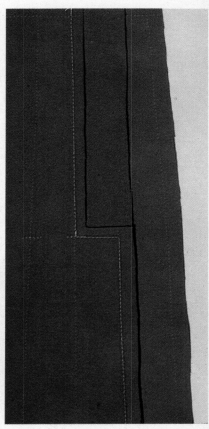

1 Having traced the lines, mark the hem, the pleat fold, and placement lines with basting. Sew the basting stitches up to about 15 cm (6") above the hem as illustrated. Remember that the lines must be marked as accurately as possible.

Baste the pleat pattern pieces together along the seam lines, right sides together. Use small stitches to the cross mark which indicates the point at which the pleat hangs free, and larger stitches for the length of the fold and meeting lines. Sew to approximately 10 cm (4") above the hem. Press the pleats down carefully on the right side with a damp cloth toward the side or the center.

2 Stitch the seams to the cross marks and fasten the ends securely. Stitch across horizontally to the seam as shown in illustration above, then stitch down to approximately 10 cm (4") above the hem and secure the ends firmly. Remove the basting threads.

When working with woolen fabrics, it is advisable to cut away the upper layer of the fabric of the pleat to 1.5 cm ($\frac{5}{8}$") from the seam. (See the illustration above again.) This reduces the bulk considerably. The remainder of the fabric will hold the pleat at the waist and prevent it from sagging. When top-stitching the pleat, leave 0.5 cm ($\frac{1}{4}$") behind the stitching line. If using a thin fabric like silk, there is no need to cut away the pleat.

3 Before the pleat seams are finished, work the lower part of each section, or each final few inches above the hem.

Baste the hem, making sure the sections are all exactly the same measurement. The hem edge of the inner fold line is marked a little higher on the pattern so that the hem does not hang down, and this makes the hem a little bit deeper on these lines. Baste the hem 1 cm ($\frac{3}{8}$") up from the cut edge and press out any fullness with a damp cloth. If using a fabric where the fullness will not press out satisfactorily, make a series of tucks along the edge instead. Remove the basting threads. Turn in the seam allowances so that they are not visible on the right side, press, and then finish the edges. Turn up the hem and sew in place with slip stitch. Press the hem edge once more. Do not remove the basting stitches on the fold lines and placement lines yet.

5 Finish the seam allowances by either zigzag stitching them together by machine, or overcasting by hand. Press the seams over strips of brown paper to prevent ridges forming.

The basting stitches mark the pleats for pressing. Join the open ends of the seams around the bottom of the skirt. Begin by securing the bottom edges together, matching them as precisely as possible, and then baste upward to the end of the stitching. Stitch the seams slowly and carefully. Baste the pleats down on the placement lines and press to set the folds. Remove the basting threads and steam the pleats on the right side with a damp cloth. To prevent ridges, insert strips of brown paper under the folds of the pleats.

4 Cut across the corners of the seam allowances along the hem. Overcast with small stitches so the corners do not hang down.

6 Top-stitching pleats serves two useful functions. Not only is it extremely decorative, adding a trim professionalism to the garment, but flat pleats are more slimming than loose pleats. Accuracy is vital! You can vary the effect simply by using a contrasting thread color. You can also vary the size of the stitches or the width of the seam. Experiment with a variety of threads for a whole range of differing effects. If you use buttonhole twist, always remember to load the bobbin with regular sewing thread.

Jeans to fit and flatter

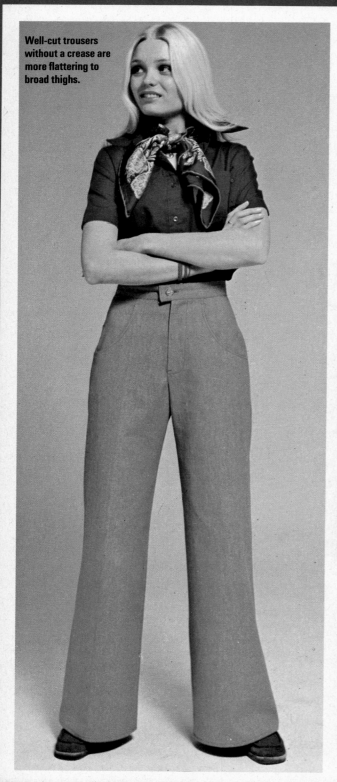

Well-cut trousers without a crease are more flattering to broad thighs.

Not everyone can buy ready-to-wear jeans that really fit and they are very difficult to alter successfully. This is why we have designed a pattern for homemade jeans — you can make them fit at the really vital points such as the waist, hips, and thighs. Sizes A to E are given on the pattern sheet. Choose the size and look that suits you best.

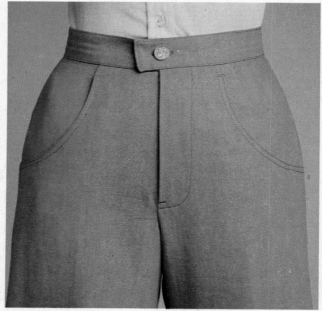

Double top-stitching on patch pockets is smart and flattering.

This detail shows the waistband and back yoke of style 1.

Style 2 is for these slim-fitting jeans. The shape is slender and should only be worn by those with narrow hips and slim legs. They have all the characteristics of jeans and will fit well. Manufactured jeans often stand away at the waist because they have been designed for men rather than women, but our styles have a shaped yoke which clings to the female figure.

These jeans look as if they have been molded to the figure. This is because they have been made to measure and fitted carefully.

The photograph above shows the narrow fit and the top-stitching on the back yoke and pocket. This back pocket is designed to emphasize the line of the style.

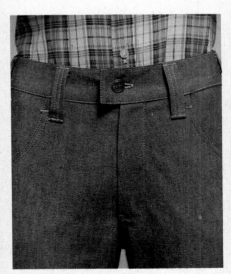

Note the loops on the waistband and the wide zipper placket. These are both features of men's jeans, so the styling is as near the original design as possible.

Cut-away pocket

The cut-away pocket is easy to make and it is often used for both trousers and skirts. The open edges of the pockets are curved or slanted for decoration and ease of use.

These cut-away pockets start at the waist on the front of the garment and curve around to the side seams. If using a thin fabric, the pocket lining can be made in the same material as the garment, but when using thicker fabrics, it is advisable to cut these pieces from lining fabric. In this way the pocket will not be as bulky, but will wear well.

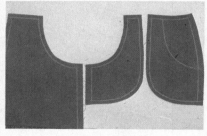

1 In the illustration above you can see the three pattern pieces which make up the pocket: these are the garment front with a cut away edge, the pocket front lining, and the pocket back. Before cutting out the pieces, transfer the outlines and all relevant signs and markings with tailor's chalk. Remember to add all the seam allowances as instructed. Mark the placement lines with a tracing wheel where indicated on the pattern. The pocket edge on the front must lie exactly on the placement line of the back part when finished, so mark with basting stitches. If you are using a wool or loosely-woven fabric, the top edge of the pocket should be strengthened with a shaped piece of interfacing basted to the wrong side of the garment front.

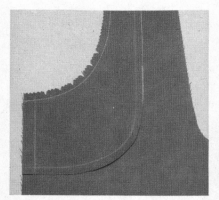

2 Place the pocket lining on the pocket edge of the garment piece, right sides together, matching all markings and lines. Stitch the pocket along the marked line at the top edge of the two pieces from the waistline edge down to the side seam.

Trim the seam allowances to 0.5 cm ($\frac{1}{4}$"). If you wish to top-stitch the pocket edge, trim the seam allowance closer to the stitching line to reduce the bulk.

Clip the curve so that the pocket lies flat after turning and the curve is as even as possible.

<u>Hint:</u> The edge will lie even flatter if you trim the seam allowance with pinking shears.

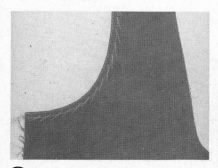

3 Turn the pocket lining to the inside and baste the curved edge with diagonal basting stitches. Press the edge with a damp cloth. It is now ready for top-stitching. By using a variety of thread weights, contrasting colors, and different stitch lengths, it is possible to achieve a wide range of effects. It is vital that top-stitching is as accurate as possible, so any irregularity must be unpicked and stitched again. Practice on a scrap of fabric before you begin.

4 Place the garment front on top of the pocket back, right sides together, and pin in place. Check that the curved edge of the garment front is lying along the marked line on the pocket back from the waist to the side seam. Trim the seam allowances evenly and finish them together with either a machine zigzag stitch or overcasting by hand.

On the inside of the garment, the pocket should look as above.

5 This is how the pocket will look on the right side. The pocket will hang freely inside the skirt or trousers, but is supported by being stitched into the waist and side seams.

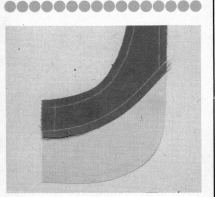

For jeans: a wide fly placket

On jeans and nearly all men's pants the zipper is inserted with a wide fly placket overlap. The overlap is cut as part of the front piece, but the underlap is cut separately.

6 When using thicker fabrics such as wool, partially line the pocket in a thinner fabric to reduce the bulk.
Two pattern pieces are provided for this purpose on the pattern; cut the top section of the pocket lining in self fabric and the lower section in suitable lining fabric.

Hint: Be sure to use a strong, tightly-woven fabric for the pocket. Lightweight lining fabrics will not withstand the normal wear of jeans. Be sure to ask for suitable pocket lining fabric at your local store.

7 Stitch together the two parts of the lining along the marked line. Clip into the seam allowance of the lining along the curve so that the piece will lie flat after pressing. Press the seam allowances toward the pocket lining and then continue making the pocket as described.

The underlap is a strip of fabric approximately 3–4 cm ($1\frac{1}{8}''$–$1\frac{5}{8}''$) wide times the length of the zipper opening. The bottom corners are rounded. Stitch the rounded corners of the underlap and overlap facing pieces together, right sides up, leaving the long edges open at this stage. Press flat. Stitch the crotch seam up to the opening for the zipper. Turn under the overlap facing on the left front along the marked line. Press. Push the seam allowance out slightly on the right front – about 0.5 cm ($\frac{1}{4}''$) – and press neatly. This edge must lie close to the teeth of the zipper. Open the zipper and baste in place with the zipper tape between the right edge and the underlap. Stitch close to the edge. Close the zipper. Place the left edge of the overlap on the center line and pin the other half of the zipper to the facing only. Open zipper and stitch to the facing. Top-stitch facing to the front.

1 Place the edge of the zipper tape along the cut edge of the underlap. Stitch with machine zigzag stitch to join the two layers together.

2 Place the underlap with the attached zipper tape under the right edge of the zipper opening. Baste and stitch.

3 Stitch the other half to the facing, stitching close to the teeth, then the tape edge.

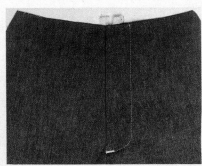

4 Top-stitch the facing to the front along the marked line. Stitch accurately for a really professional finish. Secure the bottom of the zipper with closely set zigzag stitches to strengthen this potentially weak point.

The classic shirtwaist dress

Shirtwaist dresses somehow never go out of fashion and they are always flattering and useful. Make one in pretty flowered or polka-dot cotton in sizes A to E from the enclosed pattern sheet.

The secret of the ever-popular shirtwaist dress lies in its classic lines, the fact that it suits young and old alike, and that it can be worn throughout the year. This style buttons down the front and has four large patch pockets.

The pattern for the shirtwaist dress can also be used to make this pretty spotted dress with short sleeves and an elasticized waist. This second style is made in a lightweight summer cotton, with crisp white collar and cuffs for contrast.

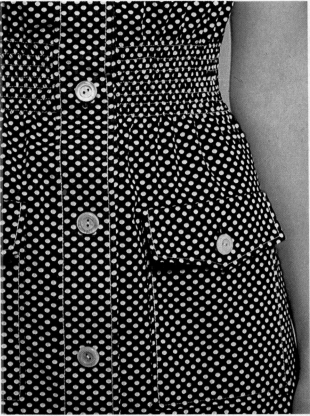

This style will be particularly flattering if you have a very small waist. The dress is top-stitched in white. Pearly buttons add the finishing touch.

The back also has features of interest. The yoke is top-stitched in white and the back is softened with gathers below the yoke.

Dots are always dramatic and popular. White collar and cuffs add a lively touch to the dress. Note that the pockets have shaped, buttoned flaps in self-fabric.

Rolled collar

It is vital to be as neat and tidy as possible when dressmaking, especially when making a collar. You need to be precise and patient to develop a flair for working in this way. Here we show you how to make blouse and dress collars. <u>Note:</u> the upper collar is illustrated in green and the under collar in beige.

The size of the upper collar is all-important if it is to fit well. The upper collar should be larger than the under collar so that it rolls away from the neck without pulling or creasing. Our pattern for the upper collar is designed to be used with the fabric suggested in the pattern. If you use an alternative fabric, remember to add or subtract fabric so that it will roll properly. Note also that the difference in size between the upper and under collar increases with the thickness of the fabric. Stitch the collar sections with the grain, starting at the center and stitching toward each end and overlapping stitches at the center.

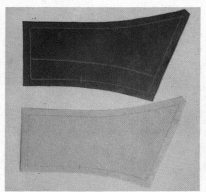

1 Place pattern pieces for upper and under collar on fabric, placing arrows on the straight of the grain for a bias cut. Add seam allowances of 1.5 cm ($\frac{5}{8}$″) and cut out. Most collars need some type of interfacing, so use the one suggested in the pattern. We have used a woven interfacing which must be cut to follow the weave of the fabric. Woven interfacing is particularly good as it adapts to the shape of the collar and helps it roll well. Unless otherwise directed, when using an iron-on interfacing, iron it onto the under collar. Transfer all marks to fabric and note arrow showing position of shoulder seam. Mark roll line on the upper collar. Place the halves of each collar section together, right sides facing. Pin, baste, and stitch the center seam.

2 Mark the roll line with basting stitches. Pin upper and under collar pieces together, right sides facing. Distribute excess fabric in upper collar evenly at the corners. Baste the pieces and check the collar roll.

3 Having pinned and basted the pieces together, they can be stitched. Machine-stitch the two layers together from the upper collar side. In this way you can be sure that the larger upper piece does not shift position or crease during stitching. Do not stitch the corners into too sharp a point or they will be difficult to turn. Instead, stitch diagonally across the corner with two or three small stitches as shown above. Press the collar before turning it. Press the seam allowances open, then toward the under collar.
Trim the seams to 0.5 cm ($\frac{1}{4}$″) with pinking shears and cut across the corners close to the stitching to reduce the bulk along the seams and at the corners.

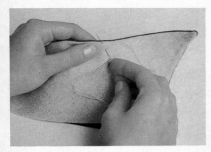

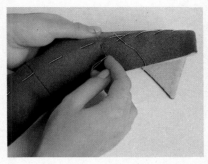

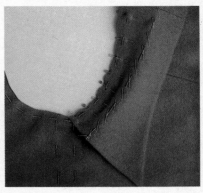

4 Turn the collar to the right side. Push the upper collar over the under collar with your left hand; the seam should not be visible from the outside. Baste the edge of the collar with diagonal basting stitches.

Now press the edge of the collar lightly with an iron on the underside. Remove the basting threads and press once more. Press cotton and wool with a damp cloth; press silk with a barely damp cloth. Always press from the side toward the center.

5 Baste the upper and under collar together along the roll line with long diagonal stitches, holding the collar over your left forefinger to achieve the correct degree of roll. The upper collar should meet the under collar on the neck edge. <u>Note:</u> It may be helpful to baste the raw edges together before the roll line.

7 Baste the upper and under collar along the neck edge on the marked seam line. Pin the collar to the neck edge of the garment, right sides up, matching all marks and inserting pins at right angles. Check the collar roll again.

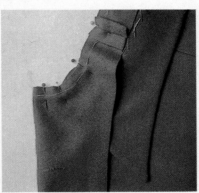

8 When using a pattern with a facing, stitch in the collar with the facing, placing the facing and collar right sides together.

A back neck facing is usually supplied if a dress is not to be lined. Join front and back facings together at the shoulder seams and press seams open. Pin facings to the neck edge, right sides together. The collar now lies between the facings and the dress as illustrated above. Stitch through all thicknesses. Trim the seam allowance back to 0.6 cm ($\frac{3}{8}$″). Turn the facings to the inside and press. Finish the edge of the facings and tack to the shoulder seams by hand.

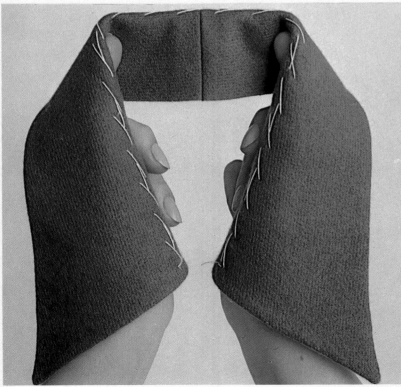

6 Hold the collar as it should look on your dress. It should not bulge, pull, or drag, and each side should be even and equal in size. If you have followed all our instructions it should fit perfectly.

Two smart tailored jackets

This smart and sporty jacket looks good in spring or autumn with skirts and pants. Sizes B–F are given on the pattern sheet.

This classic method of sewing a sleeve and cuff is strong and long-lasting.

The line of the jacket is particularly flattering because vertical lines of light-colored top-stitching carry the eye down rather than across.

Note the stitched details on the yoke and seams, and the crossed loops of this soft flannel jacket.

The yoke buttons over the patch pockets, plus top-stitching, emphasize the shape and design.

You can make this jacket in a wide variety of fabrics. Adaptations for this style are given on the enclosed pattern sheet.

Easy shirt sleeve slit opening and cuff

When making a classic shirt sleeve, the lower edge is gathered or tucked to fit the wrist with an opening so that it will slip over your hand. A cuff or band is then attached.

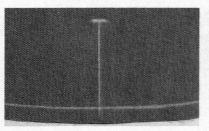

1 The slit for the opening will be marked on the pattern. Transfer the lines onto the fabric and mark the end as shown above.

Cut a facing for the opening from the same fabric. This facing must be cut on the cross or bias and should measure approximately 4 cm (1½″) wide by twice the length of the slit marked on the fabric. Now cut along the slit carefully. Pull the slit apart so that the two edges form one straight line and pin the facing along this edge, right sides up, with the facing piece underneath.

2 Stitch the facing onto the fabric from the right side. Begin at the base of the sleeve and stitch 0.5 cm (¼″) from the slit edge, decreasing the seam allowance at the marked center point of the opening. Stitch from the center out to the other side, matching the widths of the seam allowance.
Note: Because the line of stitching is so close to the raw edge of the fabric at the center point of the slit opening, it is advisable to use very small stitches or to make a second line of stitches on top of or beside the first.

3 Press the seam allowances toward the facing. Turn the facing to the right side, turn under a narrow seam allowance, and slip-stitch into place by hand. Press. Top-stitch facing close to seam on right side of sleeve.

4 To prevent the facing from twisting toward the outside, fold it at the center mark and stitch diagonally across the fold on the wrong side.
The slit opening is complete. Now attach the cuff to the edge of the sleeve. The instructions that follow are for a simple, straight cuff with a buttoned overlap.

5 Cut out the cuff and interfacing. Iron the interfacing onto one half of the cuff, extending the interfacing 1 cm (⅜″) beyond the fold line. Place the pieces right sides together and pin the cuff to the lower edge of the sleeve. Fold over the slit facing on the overlap end of the cuff. Baste. Stitch on seam line.

6 Fold the cuff, right sides together, along the marked fold line. Pin the short sides, matching the seamlines. Stitch, turning the corners to stitch the top edge of the cuff extensions. Cut the seam allowance diagonally across the corners and turn the cuff to the right side. Press carefully, pressing the seam allowances toward the cuff along the sleeve edge. The cuff should now be attached on the inside and there are two ways of doing this. Either turn under the seam allowance and slip-stitch in place by hand, or baste in place without turning in the seam allowance and secure it with top-stitching on the right side. If you use this latter method, finish the raw edge neatly by hand after top-stitching. Finally, make a buttonhole where marked on the overlap. Sew button to underlap.

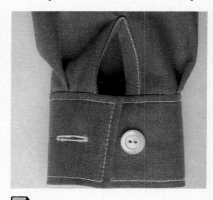

7 The photograph above shows the slit opening and attached cuff. Note that there is a tuck of excess fabric on each side.

Classic shirt sleeve slit opening and placket

This method for working a slit opening on a classic shirt sleeve is more difficult and requires patience and precision. The resulting look is both smart and sporty.

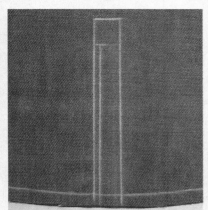

1 The slit for the opening and the line for the overlapping strip should be transferred to each sleeve.

Cut out the under and overlapping strips on the straight of the grain. The underlap piece should be 4 cm (1½″) wide and measure the length of the slit plus 2 cm (¾″). The overlap piece should be about 6 cm (2½″) wide times the length of the slit plus 4 cm (1½″).

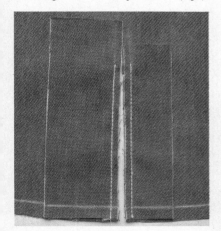

2 Pin both strips, right sides facing, to the wrong side of the sleeve, along the slit line so that their edges meet on the line. The overlap must lie on the side closest to the slit as shown in the first photograph.

Stitch each strip 0.5 cm (¼″) from the edge, stitching from the top to the bottom of the slit. Cut along the slit line with a sharp pair of scissors, snipping diagonally into the sleeve fabric at the last stitch on each side to form a small triangle.

3 Turn the underlap to the right side of the sleeve. Turn under a narrow seam allowance and fold the underlap in half so that it is about 1 cm (⅜″) wide. Top-stitch close to the edge.
Turn the overlap to the right side of the sleeve. Turn under a narrow seam allowance and fold in half so that the underlap is 2 cm (¾″) wide. Beginning at the top end of the slit opening, top-stitch close to the edge.

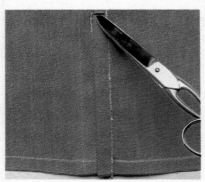

4 Turn the sleeve to the wrong side and turn under the diagonally-cut seam allowance edges which form triangles.

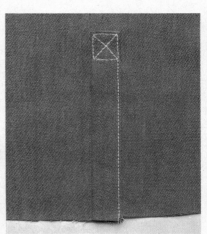

5 Turn the sleeve back to the right side. Place the overlap over the underlap and turn under the top cut ends. Pin and baste into place and finally top-stitch with a cross within a square to reinforce the opening.

6 The photograph shows the classic shirt sleeve slit opening. Attach cuff as for other type, but do not turn under slit facing.

Just cut out and iron on...

ppliqué these fabric motifs with
ending net and save yourself all
e sewing! The motifs will add a
uch of whimsy to jeans and
ckets or decorative scatter
shions and covers. Use the
otifs in more delicate fabrics to
decorate tablecloths, mats and
runners for festive occasions. The
motifs can be traced actual size
but the shapes are simple enough
to be enlarged easily. All kinds and
weights of fabric can be used to
give more unusual effects.

Appliqué is great fun, and with bonding net it's no trouble at all. The bonding net binds two fabrics together securely so that you do not need a needle and thread.

Making the motifs

Trace the motif and transfer onto the paper side of the bonding net with dressmaker's carbon paper. Place the adhesive side of the bonding net onto the wrong side of the motif fabric and press firmly down for 2–4 seconds with an iron at the heat setting for wool. The bonding net will adhere to the fabric and the motif can be cut out with a sharp pair of scissors. Allow it to cool for about 1 minute, then lift the paper backing from the bonding net and press the motif temporarily onto the background fabric—cushion, tablecloth, blouse, etc. Complete the process by pressing the motif firmly with a damp cloth for about 10 seconds. Let the piece lie flat for at least 10 minutes before testing that it has adhered properly. The motif should now be fixed firmly in place.

This is all you have to do to give new life to all kinds of dull household items and clothes.

Hint: A quick festive idea for Christmas — make a circular cloth decorated with little apples, Father Christmas figures, bright birds, or fir trees to put under the Christmas tree. For special presents, wrap them in fabric decorated with colorful iron-on motifs.

For Easter, improvise with colored eggs, spring flowers, or birds on a dainty tablecloth.

Children will love this fanciful little bird. Iron it onto curtains or cushions to brighten the nurs

This blustery general is a humorous figure to use as a wall hanging. Have fun choosing bright scraps from your favorite leftover fabrics.

Jolly Father Christmas figures and Christmas trees will be family favorites year after year. They are decorative, quick to make, and look very festive.

New life for leather leftovers

You will need very little leather for these braided belts. Remnants are ideal, provided that they are long enough, and we have used various types of leather to give a range of belts for all occasions. The belts are 3 cm (1¼″) wide (shown larger than actual size in the photograph).

Here are five braided belts, each made in a different leather and color to show you how versatile they are. They are made from leather remnants in long strips. Shiny silver or white looks glamorous for evening wear, a soft, delicate suede enhances a plain day dress, while a smooth, sporty leather in a strong color is the perfect accessory for pants.

Materials Required:
Buckle. Leather glue. Leather punch. Strip of leather or suede at least 12 cm (4¾″) wide. This width enables you to make

the ends of the belt from the remainder of the leather after cutting out the zigzag strips. For the required length, take your waist measurement and subtract 15 cm (5¾"). This is the length of the braided part.

Choosing a buckle

Choose a buckle to match the belt in both style and color. Buckles are available in a range of sizes, colors, shapes, and prices at most needlework shops and large stores. Make sure that your buckle is not too heavy for the leather, otherwise it will pull down at the waist.

Hint: Before cutting into an expensive leather or suede, try making your first belt from a cheaper leather. When this one proves successful and you feel you have had a little practice, go on to a more ambitious belt — in silver leather for example. It is worth making several, as home-made belts are cheaper than ones you buy and you will have the added satisfaction of wearing a smart accessory you have made yourself.

◀ **Silver leather, although rather expensive, is very elegant. The narrow silver buckle matches the belt beautifully.**

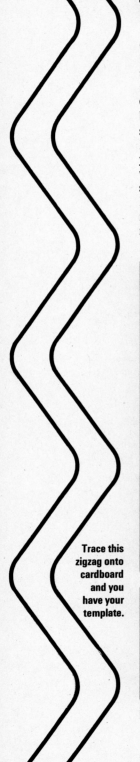

Braiding and finishing a belt

Choose the leather for the belt carefully. Don't use a thick leather or you will be unable to cut it with scissors. On the other hand, it must be firm, otherwise it will stretch quickly with wear. Pull the leather slightly and you will be able to feel whether it stretches out of shape too easily.

Practice cutting, top-stitching, and punching holes on remnants of leather first for professional-looking results.

Trace this zigzag onto cardboard and you have your template.

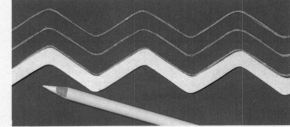

1 Trace the zigzag pattern (at left) onto heavy paper or cardboard and cut it out for the template. Draw around it on the wrong side of the leather with a pointed white pencil for dark colors or a lead pencil for light colors, extending it to the length required. 4 pencil lines = 3 strips.

◀**2** Cut out the strips carefully with scissors. Place them one on top of the other as shown and tape the ends together. The strips will automatically fall into place when being braided.

3 For the end of the belt, cut two leather strips 2.8 x 15 cm ($1\frac{1}{8}''$ x $5\frac{3}{4}''$). Trim the ends of the braided strip and stick the layers together with glue. Place the two pieces together wrong sides together, catching in one end of the braided strip. Top-stitch all around the edge and punch a neat row of holes with a leather punch.

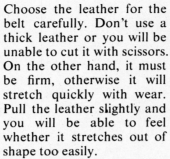

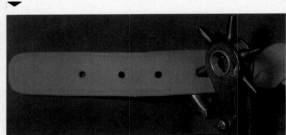

4 For the buckle end, cut a strip of leather measuring 2.8 x 18 cm ($1\frac{1}{8}''$ x $7''$). Top-stitch the long sides. In the center, make a hole for the prong, enlarging it with a small cut. Fold the strip in half around the buckle, and glue the ends together, catching in the braided strip. Stitch across the end twice.

Brushed-fabric
jacket

I like it!

A small
child
will love
this soft
and fuzzy
little
jacket.

Size: Pattern is for a child 104 cm (41") tall with a 58 cm (23") chest.

Materials Required: Brushed fabric: 75 cm ($\frac{7}{8}$ yd), 140–160 cm ($55\frac{1}{8}$– 63") wide. Cotton braid: 3 m ($2\frac{3}{4}$ yds), 3 cm ($1\frac{1}{4}$") wide. 3 large hooks and eyes (fur hooks preferably). Sewing thread to match.

Drawing the pattern

Draw a grid of squares on large sheets of paper, each square measuring 4 x 4 cm ($1\frac{5}{8}$ x $1\frac{5}{8}$"). Make dots where the contours of the pattern pieces cross the lines and squares. Join all the dots and you have an actual-size paper pattern. Transfer all marks, arrows, etc. Trace separate pocket pattern piece and then cut out all pattern pieces. Keep pattern for future use.

Cutting the pieces

Cut this type of fabric from single rather than double layers, so make a complete pattern for the back. For the sleeves and fronts, make two pattern pieces so that you don't accidentally have two right. or two left pieces.

Add a 1.5 cm ($\frac{5}{8}$") seam allowance on shoulder, side, armhole, and sleeve seams. The remaining edges of the front, back, and sleeves do not require seam allowances as they are to be bound with braid (see the photograph at left). The pocket and collar should have a 2 cm ($\frac{3}{4}$") seam allowance. Cut all

Bind the edges with a brightly colored braid which contrasts with the fabric. Close the front with fur hooks and eyes.

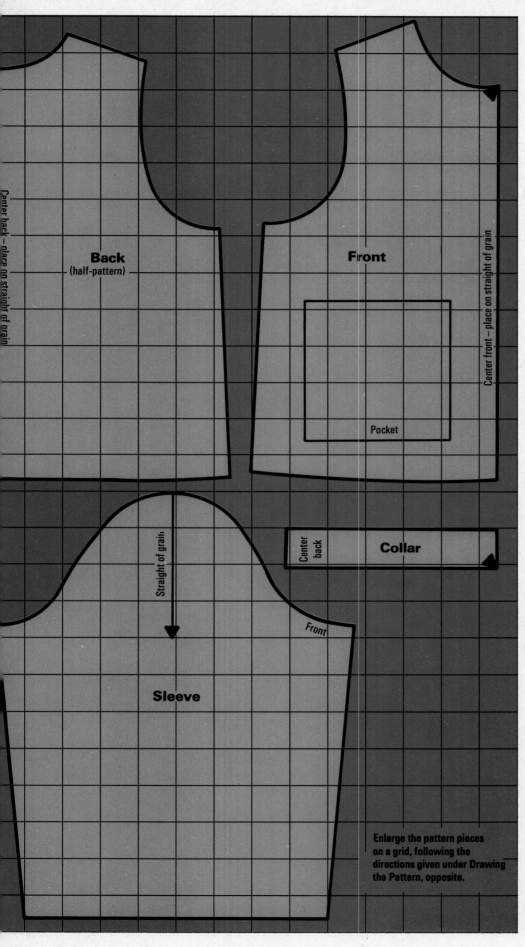

Center back – place on straight of grain

Back
(half-pattern)

Front

Center front – place on straight of grain

Pocket

Straight of grain

Center back

Collar

Straight of grain

Front

Sleeve

Enlarge the pattern pieces
on a grid, following the
directions given under Drawing
the Pattern, opposite.

the pieces with the pile running in the same direction (from top to bottom). Cut two pockets. Place the pattern piece for the stand-up collar onto a fold of fabric and cut one.

Sewing the jacket

First baste all the seams, as this type of fabric tends to shift position easily while stitching.

Join the shoulder and side seams, then trim and finish the seam allowances. Stitch the collar to the neck edge, finish the seam allowance, and press it up toward the collar. Join the sleeve seams, and insert the sleeves into the armholes, matching the grain line of the sleeve to the shoulder seam and the sleeve seam to the side seam. Finish raw edges.

Bind the edges with braid as follows: Pin and baste one edge of the braid 0.5 cm ($\frac{1}{4}$") from the fabric edge on the wrong side. Stitch 1 cm ($\frac{3}{8}$") from the edge. Turn the braid over the fabric edge neatly, fold it under, and baste to the stitching line before sewing neatly in place by hand. On corners, fold the braid over and hand-sew together neatly and firmly. At the sleeve edges, cut the braid to the correct length and join into a circle before stitching as described above. Stitch braid to the top edge of the pockets and then turn under and baste the other edges. Pin the pockets to the marked lines on the fronts and sew in place by hand. Sew on hooks and eyes so that they are approximately 0.2 cm ($\frac{1}{8}$") inside each edge.

Stitch first and then embroider

A touch of girlish humor

Fashion-conscious girls will love these simple-to-make and easy-to-wear little vests. Chamois washing leather is soft, supple, very easy to sew, and ideal for these designs. Decorate them with amusing embroidered motifs.

Our leather vests are for 10- and 13-year-olds with an average height of 140 cm (55″) and 158 cm (62¼″). See the two styles on the opposite page. Washing leathers can be bought from any good hardware shop or store. Choose leathers that are relatively firm as chamois stretches easily. Keep the vests clean by washing in warm soapy water, then rinsing and drying in the open air. Avoid direct sunlight, heat, and chemicals or the leather will become hard.

The pattern for the 10-year-old is cut quite straight and is really simple to make. Cut the edges with pinking shears so that they do not need to be finished later.

Embroider the yoke after stitching.

342

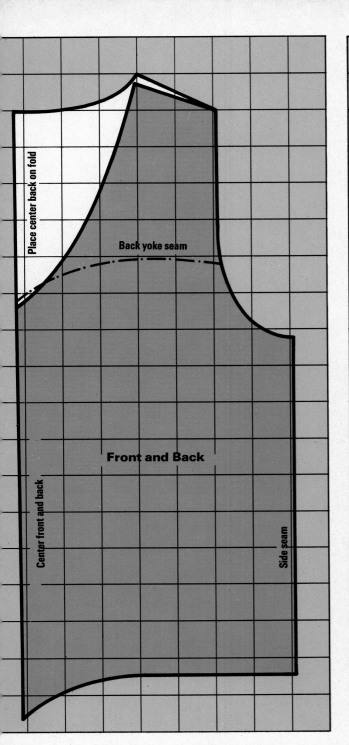

Place center back on fold

Back yoke seam

Center front and back

Front and Back

Side seam

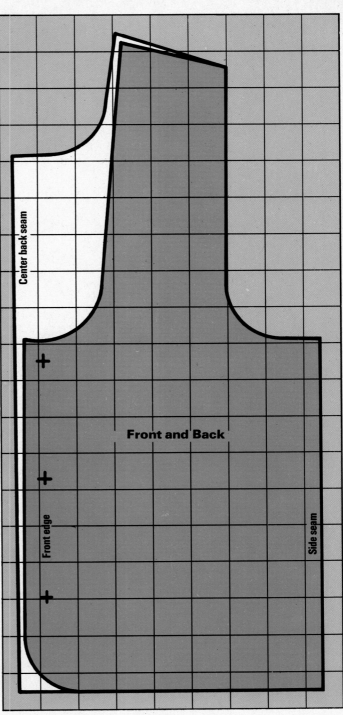

Center back seam

Front edge

Front and Back

Side seam

Enlarging the pattern

Here you can see the scaled-down patterns for the two designs. On the left is the pattern for a 10-year-old, chest 70 cm (27½″) and height 140 cm (55″); on the right is the pattern for a 13-year-old, chest 79 cm (31¼″) and height 158 cm (62¼″).

If you want to make either of the waistcoats you must enlarge the pattern above using the following method: Draw a grid 22.5 cm x 47.5 cm (9″ x 19″) on a large sheet of paper. Mark it off in squares measuring 2.5 cm x 2.5 cm (1″ x 1″). Now mark all the points where the contour lines of the pattern pieces cross the grid lines. Join all these points and you will have full-sized pattern pieces. After use, store the pattern in a clearly marked paper envelope so that you can use it again later.

The snail is embroidered with stranded cotton using satin stitch. The body is orange and the shell is in shades of red.

The row of caterpillars is worked

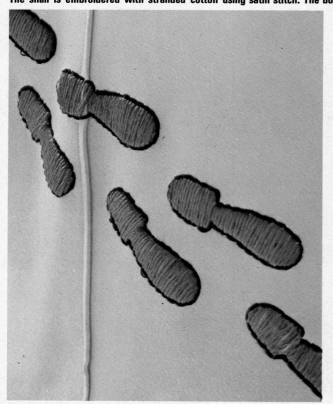

Satin stitch footprints in green are edged with black in backstitch.

The birds are worked in stranded cotton. Use yellow, orange, red, and pink satin stit

Here is an array of colorful motifs which
you can embroider with simple stitches —
straight, stem, satin, and backstitch.
Use stranded cotton and a leather needle,
taking care not to place the stitches
too close together or the leather may split.

the back yoke using six strands of stranded cotton. The head and legs are in red, the nose, eyes and ears are in black, and the body is in three shades of green.

r the bodies and black straight stitch and stem stitch for the legs, eyes and feathers.

Embroider the gay umbrellas with all six strands in blue, yellow, and red.

Sewing

10-year-old design

This pattern is for an average 10-year-old: height 140 cm (55″) and chest 70 cm (27½″).

Cutting out: Take the pattern with you when buying the leather so that you buy the right size.

Before cutting out, try on the pattern by making a paper or muslin pattern. Make any alterations necessary on this rather than on the leather which marks easily. Trace the outlines of the pattern pieces onto the leather with a fine pencil as lightly as possible.

Seam allowances: Add 0.5 cm (¼″) on shoulders, the sides of the back and the upper edge of the back. Cut these edges with straight-edged shears. Cut all other edges with pinking shears.

Sewing: Stitch the side seams, shoulder seams, and the back yoke with the pinked edges overlapping the straight edges. Use paper clips to hold the seams together during stitching as pins or basting would mark the leather.

13-year-old design

This pattern is for an average 13-year-old: height 158 cm (62¼″) and chest 79 cm (31¼″).

Cutting out: As above.

Seam allowances: Add 0.5 cm (¼″) on sides and shoulders of back and on the right side of the center back seam. Cut all other edges along seam lines. For the front fastening, cut six strips measuring 0.5 cm (¼″) wide by 18 cm (7¼″) long.

Sewing: Overlap and stitch the side and shoulder seams and center back seam. Secure the pieces with paper clips as you work to avoid marking the leather with pins or basting. Sew the strips to the front edges, strengthening with small squares of leather on the inside.

This second style is for a 13-year-old, height 158 cm (62¼″). Your daughter can fasten it with strips of leather or wear it open. Notice how well the umbrella motifs fit the shape of the pattern piece and add a decorative touch to what is basically a very simple design.

◄ **The positioning of the motifs is entirely up to you. Here the footsteps march diagonally across.**

A finishing touch...

Add these amusing motifs to our washing leather vests or to anything which needs an extra special touch.

Embroidery

Hemstitch is now rarely used in its original form to simply sew a hem. Instead, it is used as a decorative stitch in drawn-thread embroidery.

Drawnwork to enhance beautiful linens

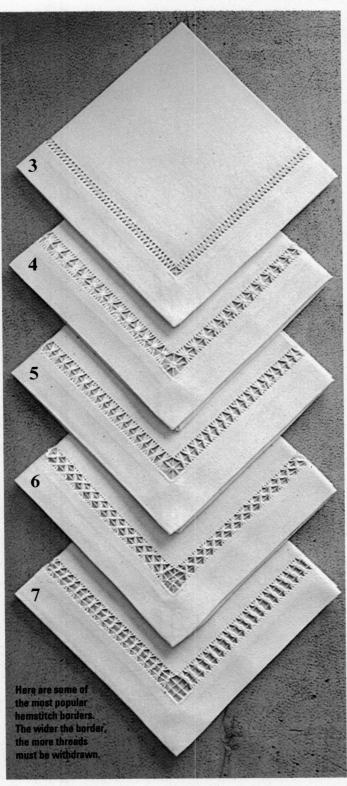

Here are some of the most popular hemstitch borders. The wider the border, the more threads must be withdrawn.

Hemstitch and needle-weaving are the two techniques used in drawnwork.

It gives a distinctive decorative finish to table linens, clothes, and accessories.

Size: The finished size of the place mats is 30 x 40 cm (11¾" x 15¾"). The napkins are 30 cm (11¾") square. Cut out the pieces along the grain of the fabric to measure 40 x 50 cm (15¾" x 19¾") and 40 cm (15¾") square respectively. This includes twice the 2.5 cm (1") hem allowance to make a double turning. The first turning can be slightly narrower if necessary.

Materials Required: Medium-weight even-weave linen. White stranded embroidery cotton (use 4 strands or match the thickness of the linen threads).

Drawing the threads
Mark the position of the hem and the drawn-thread areas on the wrong side of the fabric with pins or fine pencil lines. The outer drawn threads will be about 7.5 cm (3") in from the edges. The width of the drawn-thread areas on Nos. 1–3 is 0.5 cm (¼"), on Nos. 4–7, 1 cm (⅜").

Draw out the threads. On the place mats, the drawn threads cross at the corners and extend to the edges of the fabric, so draw the threads from the outside inward. On the napkins and inside the place mats, where the drawn threads do not extend to the edges, cut the outer thread in the middle and draw out to both sides as far as the marks. Continue withdrawing threads until the open area is the required width. Either weave in the ends of the threads invisibly or cut off the fabric thread ends and finish the edges with buttonhole or overcasting stitch. Miter the corners; turn under the hem.

Embroidering

Work hemstitch along the top and bottom of the drawn-thread areas. In Nos. 2 and 3, group four threads together; for the rest, group three threads together. In No. 1 use ladder hemstitch. The squares inside the border are worked in overcast bars. No. 2 is overcast ladder hemstitch. No. 3 is zigzag hemstitch. For Nos. 4–7, the thread groups are tied in a decorative way. Three groups are connected in Nos. 5 and 7, four in Nos. 4 and 6.

Fill in the empty corners on the narrow designs with crossed threads. The larger corners are filled in with several crossed threads in a design matching the style of the work. Do not pull these threads too tight.

Making the hem

Turn under the hem before working the outer row of hemstitch. The hem edge is then caught in with the stitching. On the place mats, work the small designs inside the main border areas, then work the border and the hem. At the corners, the hem-stitching or overcasting will be worked over three layers of fabric.

Drawn-thread embroidery

Plain hemstitch

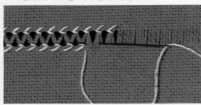

1 Work from left to right on the wrong side of the fabric. Pass the needle from right to left behind the required number of threads.

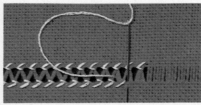

2 Insert the needle at the same point, going two fabric threads down. For ladder hemstitch, repeat on the other side with the same groups.

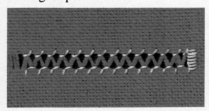

3 Zigzag hemstitch (right side): work over an even number of threads. On opposite side, each group is made up of $\frac{1}{2}$ the threads from two adjacent groups.

4 Corners are finished with close buttonhole stitch. To fill corners, stretch the thread over crosswise several times and buttonhole-stitch over middle to form a cross.

Hemstitch variation

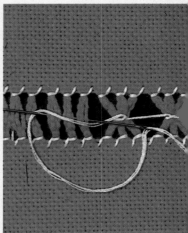

1 Gather several groups threads together and fasten the with a slip knot. To do this, form loop with the thread and, with t needle above the loop, pass behind the groups. Bring it o inside the loop and pull the thre carefully to tighten the knot so th the distance between the grou is equal. You can work this stit from either side of the fabric.

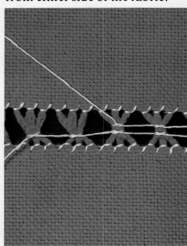

2 Work two rows of slip knots the same way. Work from right left and from either side of t fabric at equal intervals. Napk border No. 7 is worked with th decorative stitch.

Mark the length and width of the drawn-thread areas on the wrong side of the fabric. Draw out the threads, then embroider the remaining threads with hemstitch variations.

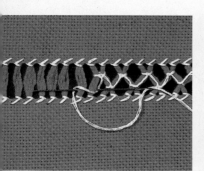

3a For a double zigzag effect, thread groups are joined in a staggered formation. Because the working thread runs from one slip knot to another, the stitches must be worked from the wrong side. Pass the needle behind two thread groups about one third up from the base to begin this stitch.

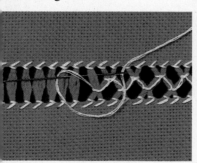

3b Loop the thread up and around to form another slip knot, passing the needle behind the last group and the next group along, about two thirds up from the base. Pull the knot tight.

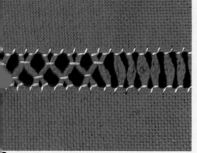

3c The double zigzag as seen from the right side of the fabric.

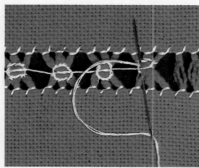

4 Join several groups of threads with slip stitches, then work small circles in the center in stem stitch or backstitch.

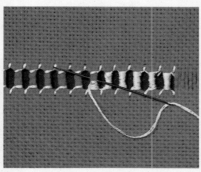

5 The groups of threads in ladder hemstitch can be closely overcast to form wrapped bars.

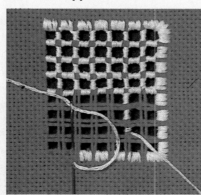

6 For a grid design, first overcast the raw edges closely. Then overcast the remaining horizontal and vertical threads firmly to form wrapped bars, giving a trellis effect.

Forming hem and corners

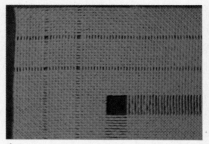

1 Allow three times the required width of the hem (for the double turning and the front). Mark the fold lines on heavy linen by drawing a thread along them and on fine linen with a pencil line. Withdraw the threads.

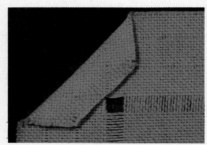

2 To miter the corners neatly, fold them in once so that the marked lines meet. Cut off the corner points evenly at the inner turning line.

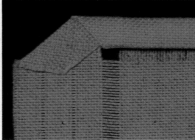

3 Now turn the hem under twice and baste it in place. Slip-stitch the mitered corners together. Catch in the edges of the hem as you work the hemstitch.

Our alphabet is delicate and ornate in white stranded embroidery cotton. Each letter
beautifully embroidered in stem stitch and padded satin stitch to make it stand ou

Alphabet in stem stitch and satin stitch

Take a letter...

mbroidered script initials look smart and elegant on blouses, shirts, dresses, scarves, andkerchiefs, and bed linen, and never go out of fashion!

A B C D

I J K L

O R S T

Y Z

Interlocking monograms in relief are most effective worked in white on white. Pillow cases, the turn-back on sheets, or handkerchiefs will all have a more elegant look.

1

2

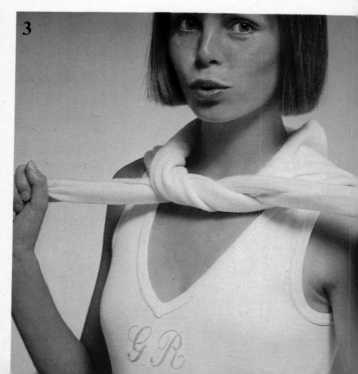

3

1 Something special: an initial on the beret and a decorative motif on the matching scarf.

2 Embroider your initials on the corners of a blouse collar.

3 A plain T-shirt or sports shirt can be boring. Give it an individual touch with embroidered initials.

4 A man's evening scarf becomes more distinctive with an embroidered monogram.

Embroidering initials

At one time, embroidered monograms adorned a young girl's trousseau. Today, they are a dainty and individual ornamentation on clothes and accessories. The wide areas of the letters are padded with filler stitches and appear to stand out in relief from the background. For this reason, white on white is very effective.

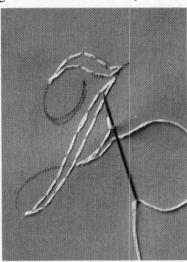

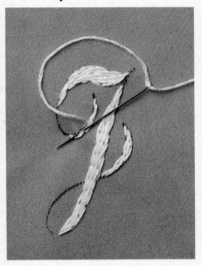

1 Preliminary stitch: Trace the outlines of the wide areas to be worked in satin stitch with closely-worked running stitches.

2 Padding stitches: Fill in the outlined areas with closely-worked running stitches to form a base for the satin stitch.

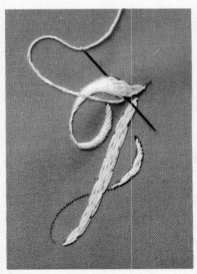

3 Satin stitch: Embroider over the padded areas with a slanting satin stitch, using two strands of stranded cotton.

4 Stem stitch: The fine lines of the letters are worked in stem stitch. The finished letter appears to stand out in relief.

Trace a letter

Embroidered monograms will look sma[r] and elegant on everything from blouses shirts, scarves, and berets to bed linen and handkerchiefs. Worked in white in stem stitch and padded satin stitch for a raised effect, they add a distinctive touch to your clothes and accessories.

Create a wisp of a curtain

This curtain has a wonderfully light and
airy appearance. The
delicate embroidered border is worked in
drawn fabric stitches
onto loosely-woven cotton. Although it
needs a fair amount of patience and
good eyesight, the end result is breathtaking.

Size: Width about 110 cm (43").
Materials Required: For the two curtains in the width given, use stranded embroidery cotton in the following colors and quantities: 6 skeins olive, 4 skeins apricot, 3 skeins each yellow, lilac, lime green, turquoise, 2 skeins rose, 1 skein green. Metallic gold thread: 1 skein. Loosely-woven cotton in natural color: 112 cm (45") wide, in required length, plus 15 cm (6") for hems.

Preparing the fabric

Rinse the fabric in clear water, let it dry, and iron it.

Trace and transfer the lower border first 15 cm (6") above the fabric edge, repeating as many times as necessary and adding the border ends at the side edges.

Transfer the large motifs 3 cm ($1\frac{1}{8}$") above the border, about 9 cm ($3\frac{1}{2}$") apart. Alternate the Tree of Life with the other two motifs.

Transfer the small motifs in between the large ones and the narrow border 6 cm ($2\frac{1}{2}$") above the large motifs.

Working the embroidery

The basic stitches are four-sided stitch used as a surface stitch, four-sided stitch used as a drawn fabric stitch, honeycomb stitch, satin stitch, and stem stitch, with some cross-stitch. Use 4 strands of stranded cotton in the needle. The four-sided drawn fabric stitch is worked over 3 to 4 threads of the fabric.

Making the curtain

Turn up a 5 cm (2") hem twice and stitch close to the bottom edge of the wide border. Hem top and side edges. Steam the hems and the embroidery carefully on the right side.

Narrow Border: embroider the vine in stem stitch. The trefoils are outlined with stem stitch and the drawn fabric areas are filled in with four-sided stitch. Use olive for the vine, and turquoise with lilac or turquoise with apricot for the trefoils.

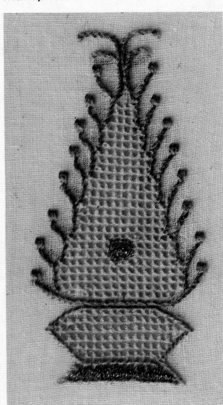

Tree of Life: the outlines are worked in stem stitch and the dots in satin stitch. The drawn fabric areas are then filled in with four-sided stitch to form an openwork trellis effect. The base is worked in satin stitch and the circle in the center in satin and stem stitch using gold thread. Colors: lilac, rose, yellow, and green.

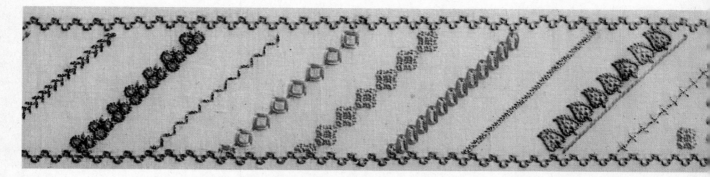

Wide Border: work the outline first in honeycomb stitch using olive stranded cotton, then work the slanting lines.

Staggered Line: work half four-sided stitch in gold thread.

Trefoils: the outlines are worked in stem stitch in turquoise and the drawn fabric areas are filled in with four-sided stitch in apricot.

Stepped Lines: work these in half four-sided stitch in gold thread.

Squares: the outer squares are worked in lime green four-sided stitch, the inner ones in apricot.

Four-flower Squares: the outline is worked in stem stitch in rose, then filled in with four-sided stitch in lime green.

Rectangles: work the outlines in apricot four-sided stitch with the vertical stitches double the length of the horizontal stitches. Fill in with satin stitch in lilac.

Gold Stripe: work horizontal satin stitch using gold thread.

Leaf Line: the diagonal line is yellow stem stitch; the leaf outline is green stem stitch filled in with four-sided stitch in yellow.

Border Ends: embroider the four-flower square as above and the line next to it in gold-thread cross-stitch.

Motif with Diamonds: the outlines are worked in stem stitch, the drawn fabric areas in four-sided stitch, and the lines at the diamond points are straight stitches. The gold stripes are worked in satin stitch and the gold crosses inside the flowers are large cross-stitches. The colors used are lime green, lilac, and apricot.

Small Motifs: the outlines are worked in stem stitch and the inner areas in four-sided stitch. The colors are rose with lime green, green with yellow, and lilac with apricot.

Clover Motif: the outlines are worked in stem stitch and the drawn fabric areas in four-sided stitch. The gold stripe is worked in satin stitch and the gold crosses inside the clover leaves can be worked as cross-stitches or four straight stitches. The colors used are lime green, olive, apricot, rose, and turquoise.

Four-sided stitch

Four-sided stitch can be varied in several ways to produce very different effects. It can be used as a border pattern or as a filling stitch. It can also be worked as a surface or a drawn fabric stitch.

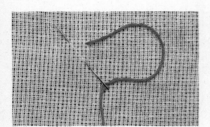

1a Four-sided stitch as a surface stitch: If using an even-weave fabric, work over 3 or 4 threads for each stitch, otherwise follow the transferred outline. Insert the needle vertically down and bring it out again diagonally to to the left. The horizontal and vertical stitch length should always be the same.

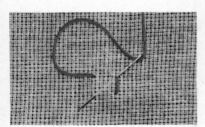

1b Insert the needle back into the top of the first stitch and bring it out diagonally down to the left. The two stitches which have now been worked form two sides of a square.

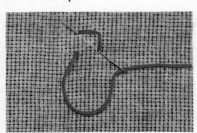

1c Insert the needle into the base of the first stitch, bringing it out diagonally up to the left. Repeat from 1a.

2 Four-sided stitch worked diagonally: First follow the steps shown in 1a to 1c. When completing the fourth side of the square, bring the needle out twice the length of one stitch to the right. This is the starting point for the next stitch.

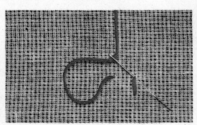

3a Half four-sided stitch worked diagonally: Begin working as described in 1a. Then insert the needle back into the top of the first stitch and bring it out diagonally down to the right. Make sure the horizontal and vertical stitches are equal.

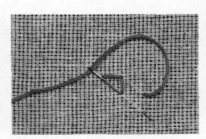

3b Insert the needle to the base of the first stitch and bring it out diagonally down to the right, below the last thread.

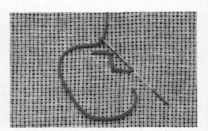

3c Continue working alternate horizontal and vertical stitches to form a stepped line.

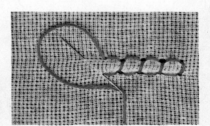

4 Four-sided stitch as a drawn fabric stitch: This is worked in the same way as 1a–1c, but the thread should be pulled firmly after each stitch so that the fabric threads are drawn apart making an openwork pattern. This is used as a filler stitch.

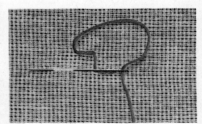

5 Honeycomb stitch: Only the first step is shown here, where the needle is inserted into the fabric and brought out horizontally to the left. Second step: bring the needle back and make another stitch in the same place. Then move up or down and work a double horizontal stitch.

Embroider a border

Add a decorative border to simple curtains. This embroidery is stunning on light and airy fabrics such as loosely-woven cotton. Traditional motifs such as the Tree of Life are worked in drawn fabric stitches in delicate colors.

Clover Motif

Border End

Border End

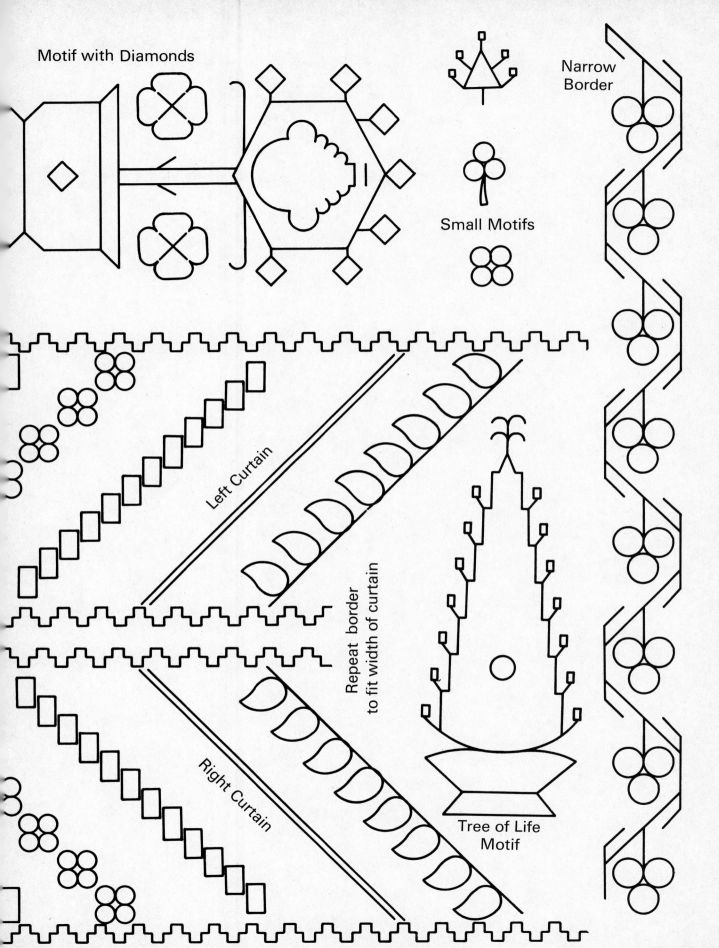

Motif with Diamonds

Narrow Border

Small Motifs

Left Curtain

Right Curtain

Repeat border to fit width of curtain

Tree of Life Motif

In reverse tent stitch

Pictures in the round

Materials Required: Stranded embroidery cotton in gold, yellow, red, green, blue, rust, pink and black. Single-thread canvas: 15 cm (6") squares of 22 threads to 2.5 cm (1"). Small tapestry frame. Round picture frames, 5 cm (2") inside diameter.

Making the pictures

Stretch the canvas on the tapestry frame. Follow the chart, using the photograph as a color guide. Work the pictures in petit point (small tent stitch), using 3 strands of stranded cotton in the needle. The stitches shown here slope in the opposite direction from normal tent stitch. To work reverse tent stitch, work from left to right and insert the needle one mesh diagonally down to the right and bring it out two meshes diagonally up to the left.

Trim the canvas to 2 cm (¾") all around the completed picture. Place it over a circle of cardboard and tape in place. Fix it into the frame with brads.

These three delicate canvaswork miniatures, inspired by ancient figure motifs, are worked in glowing colors with stranded embroidery cotton on fine single-thread canvas. Frame them with ready-made round frames, painted gold for a sumptuous look.

Each square = 1 stitch. Follow the photograph for colors

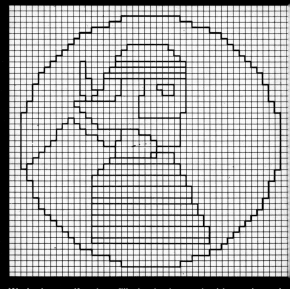

Work the motifs, then fill the background with another color

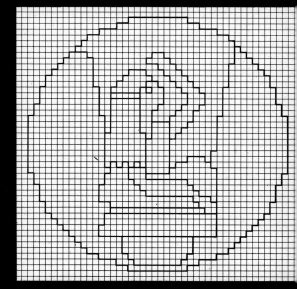

Make the background larger than the inside frame measurement

New ideas for your sofa in
A wool-saving rug technique

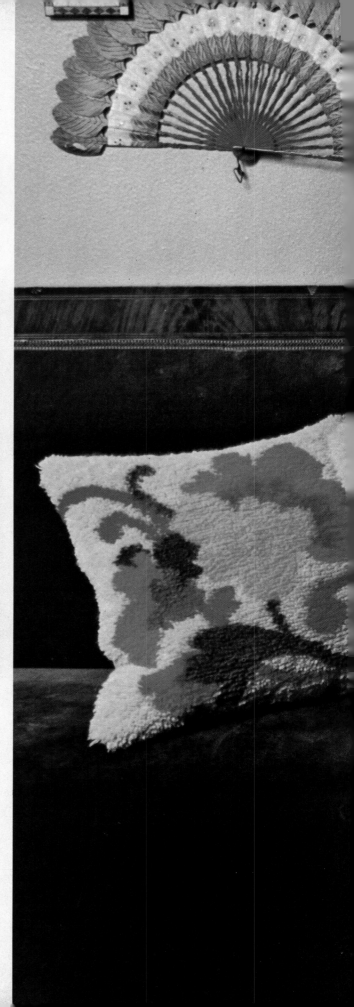

Make short-pile cushions in glowing colors with this clever knotting technique.

The short, close pile of these cushions is made by knotting tapestry wool over a pile gauge or a knitting needle onto a background of double-thread canvas. The great advantage of this particular technique is that it is an economical use of wool, as the pile is shorter than on an ordinary hooked rug.

Using this same method, you can also make other items such as wall hangings or patterned rugs as long as you use the proper materials. Tapestry yarn is ideal for cushions, but you must use thicker yarn for a rug. Whatever materials you use, the thick pile will show up the design. The height of the pile depends on the thickness of the pile gauge or knitting needle. Use a larger size for longer pile. A pile gauge measuring 1 cm ($\frac{3}{8}$″) gives a pile height of about 1.3 cm ($\frac{1}{2}$″), while a size 8 (Am) or 5 (Eng) knitting needle gives a pile height of 0.5 cm ($\frac{1}{4}$″).

As a special feature
or long sofas,
hese cushions have been
specially designed
so that when they are
placed in a row, they
orm a continuous pattern.

Here are charts for two of the set of three floral cushions. Each square represents one knot made over the pile gauge. Always begin at the lower left corner.

1 Materials you will need to m[...] the cushions: double-thread [...] canvas measuring 46 cm (18″) squ[...] with 7 holes to 2.5 cm (1″) a[...] tapestry yarn (13.7 m or 15 yd ske[...] in the required colors and quantit[...]

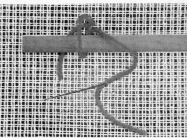

5 Use the pile gauge for the n[...] knot. Make sure the two ends of y[...] from the previous knot are point[...] downward and place the pile ga[...] horizontally on top of them. L[...] the yarn up and over to the lef[...] the pile gauge. Insert the tapes[...] needle between the pair of horizo[...] threads one square to the right of [...] first knot.

9 Always work in rows [...] from left to right and [...] from bottom to top. The [...] pile will be close and short, and [...] stand out from the canvas so tha[...] beautifully clear design is form[...] showing all the details. Follow [...] colors from the chart as you w[...] each row. Each square represe[...] one knot. For each new row, pl[...] the pile gauge over the pile from [...] row below and work the knots of [...] ferent colors as before.

Knotting over a pile gauge

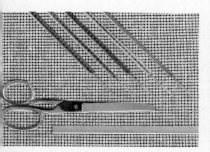

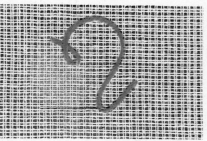

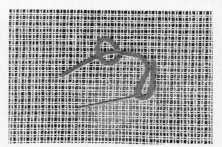

Tools you will need: a pile gauge a knitting needle (use a pile gauge cm ($\frac{3}{8}$") wide for the correct pile ngth for the cushions), scissors, d a tapestry needle with a blunt int for each yarn color.

3 To begin knotting: the first stitch is worked without the pile gauge or knitting needle. Insert the needle downward in between a pair of horizontal threads, then loop the yarn to the left over the loose end.

4 Now insert the needle under the upper horizontal thread. Pull the yarn tight to form a knot. The first knot has now been completed. All further knots are worked over the pile gauge.

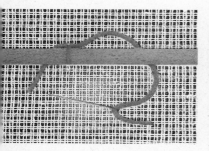

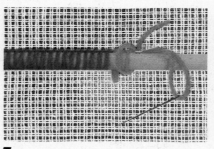

Take the yarn up and around ain in a loop to the left, insert e tapestry needle under the upper rizontal thread and pull tight. ring the yarn under the pile gauge. epeat from step 5 for the next knot.

7 When starting a new color, lay the end of the yarn under the pile gauge and begin by inserting the needle in between the horizontal threads. Make a knot as in step 4, then continue to knot as before.

8 When the pile gauge is full of knots, turn it so that it stands on its edge and pull it out, cutting the loops with a pair of sharp pointed scissors as you pull. Move it along to the right and continue knotting.

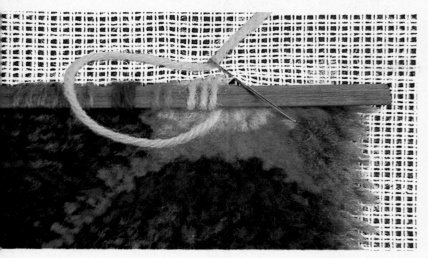

10 The chart can be enlarged onto graph paper so that it can be followed more easily. Make an envelope for the chart to serve as a row guide. Cut a piece of cardboard the width of the chart and stick a piece of stiff paper across it. As you work, push the chart down so the paper underlines the next row.

Crafts

Here is a whole pattern for one floral cushion and a quarter-pattern for the geometric repeat. Each square represents one knot made over the pile gauge. Always begin at the lower left corner.

Following the charts

The knotted designs are easy to follow from the charts. For the three floral cushions, use the charts showing the complete design, beginning at the bottom left corner. For the other cushion, a chart showing a quarter of the design is given. Begin knotting at the bottom left corner and when you reach the center of the design on the first row, work the right half as a mirror image of the left half. Continue to work to the top of the chart. Work the top half as a mirror image of the bottom half.

Making the cushions

Cut the canvas to measure just under 46 cm (18") square. This gives a cushion about 35 cm (13¾") square with a 5 cm (2") border of unworked canvas. Finish raw edges with tape or overcasting. Sew on a matching backing fabric around three sides. Insert a cushion and sew up the fourth side.

Shown below are the colors and quantities of tapestry yarn (13.7 m or 15 yd skeins) required for the three floral cushions:

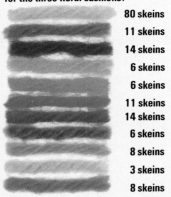

80 skeins
11 skeins
14 skeins
6 skeins
6 skeins
11 skeins
14 skeins
6 skeins
8 skeins
3 skeins
8 skeins

For the geometric-patterned cushion:

24 skeins
22 skeins
3 skeins
3 skeins
11 skeins

omething unusual for your home
Patchwork with a difference...

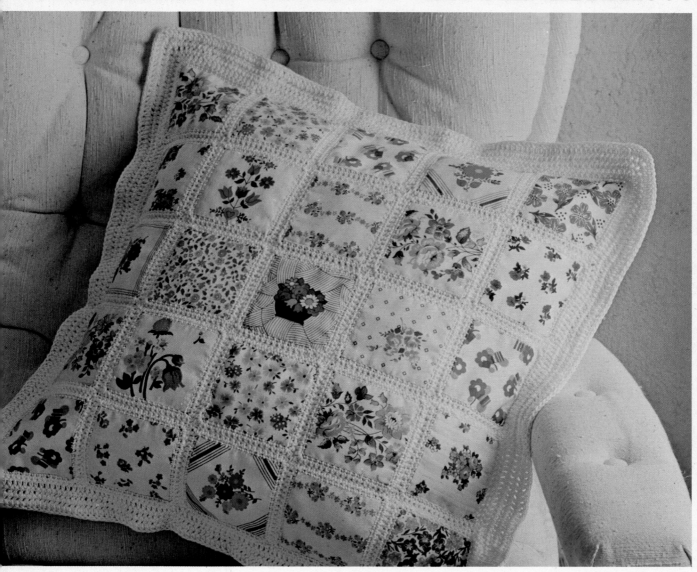

USHION

Materials Required: 25
mnants of flowered cotton
bric, each measuring 10
n (4") square; the same
umber of squares in plain
tton for backing patches.
ain cotton: 70 cm (27½")
ng, 90 cm (36") wide for
acking cushion. Interlining:
cm (11¾"), 80 cm (31½")
de. White embroidery
tton: 150 gm (6 oz).
ochet hook size C. One
shion 51 cm (20") square.

Making the cushion
Cut interlining into 25
squares, each measuring 8
x 8 cm (3⅛" x 3⅛"). Assemble squares as described,
overleaf, in Illustrations 1
and 2. Work a border in 2
rounds of single crochet.
Work the first round into the
blanket stitches and shape
corners with 2 single
crochets in the last stitch of
a side, chain 1, single
crochet into first stitch of
next side. In the second

round, work 2 single
crochets, 1 chain, 2 single
crochets into the corner
chains.
When all squares are
complete, arrange on a flat
surface. Sew the patches
into strips, then sew the
strips together. Work 5
rows of double crochets
around cushion cover,
working corners as 1 double
crochet, 1 chain, 1 double
crochet. Sew on backing;
insert cushion and close

BEDSPREAD
Materials Required: 182
remnants of flowered cotton
fabric, each measuring 12
cm (4¾") square; and 182
patches for backing. Interlining. White embroidery
cotton: 1400 gm (50 oz).
Crochet hook size C.

Making the bedspread
Cut the interlining into 10
cm (4") squares. Assemble
squares as described, overleaf, in Illustrations 1—4.

1 Place a square of inter-lining onto the wrong side of a square of fabric. Turn over edges and baste in place with long stitches as illustrated.

Note: The corners should be neat and accurate. No raw edges should show on the right side and the patch should lie completely flat. Press carefully.

2 Press under edges of a backing square with a slightly wider seam allowance to make it a little smaller than the first square. Place squares with wrong sides together, and baste. Work blanket stitch around edges, making the stitches 5mm ($\frac{1}{4}$″) apart. Do not pull stitches too tight or the crochet hook will not go through them.

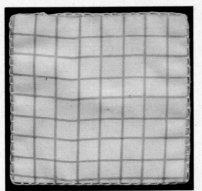

3 Work a crochet border in 2 rounds of double crochet. Work the first round into the blanket stitches and shape corners by working 2 double crochets into the last stitch of a side, chain 2, then work 2 double crochets into the first stitch of the next side. In the second round, work 2 double crochets, 1 chain, 2 double crochets into the corner chains.

4 When all 182 squares are finished, weave in the ends, then arrange them on a flat surface. Sew the arrangement together in strips, then sew the strips together. Work a crochet border around the bedspread in 2 rounds of double crochet, working 2 double crochets, 1 chain, 2 double crochets into the corner chains. Weave in all ends, so that they do not show on either side.

nd cushion

The patches are two-sided. For a reversible bedspread, try one side in floral designs and the other in plain fabrics.

Potato printing on tablecloths, place mats, napkins

Color and imagination are all you need

Colored butterflies decorate this party tablecloth. They are printed along the hem as a border and in a circle in the center. Use many colors for the wings.

Steffi

▲ Two rows of apples edge the place mat. A subtle effect is produced by using a stamp several times without dipping it in the paint.

◄ Print place cards with the same motif as the tablecloth.

Potato printing is an effective way of making pretty designs from simple shapes. The most obvious shapes to work with are straight-sided geometric ones such as squares, rectangles, triangles, stars, or bars. But with a little more care you can cut round or oval motifs into the potatoes. The effect is created by the regular repetition of the shapes, which can be placed on top of or beside each other.

Crafts

Choosing the materials

To make the stamps, choose large potatoes which are really firm and fresh. You can print onto most kinds of fabric and paper. The most suitable fabric for a tablecloth is cotton or a cotton/linen blend. Coarse weaves or very textured fabrics will distort the design. Fabric with dressing or sizing on it should be washed before being printed because part of the color will dissolve along with the dressing or sizing at the first wash and the design will become fuzzy at the edges.

Cover the working surface with a plastic cloth or a large clean sheet of paper.

For the stamp pad, stretch a piece of felt over half the area of a wooden board; the other half can be used as a cutting board for the potatoes.

Arranging motifs

Potato printing is especially decorative on place mats, napkins, tablecloths and runners, curtains, or cards, where the motif appears several times. In repeat patterns — where the motif recurs at regular intervals — mark the position of each motif with light pencil lines and a ruler. Or baste a strip of paper along the edge of the fabric, just below the border, marking on it the shapes and colors.

◀ Here are some motifs for a children's party table. They are all made up of simple shapes which you can draw and transfer onto a paper template with dressmaker's carbon paper before cutting into the potato stamp.

Materials for potato printing:

1. A small sharp knife.
2. Very fresh potatoes.
3. Permanent fabric printing colors.
4. Turpentine.
5. Several small pots for mixing paints (egg cups, yoghurt pots, etc.).
6. A glass for the turpentine – to clean the brushes between colors.
7. Fabric scraps for printing tests.
8. Inexpensive paint brushes: one for each color.
9. A fine-tipped pen.
10. White paper. Paper towels.
11. A ruler and compass for marking the position of the motifs. Scissors.
12. A clean working surface.
13. Tracing paper and dressmaker's carbon paper for transferring the motifs.
14. Pins or tacks to secure fabric.
15. Various shapes (pastry cutters, film tins, etc.)

4 Cut the potato straight down the middle, round it off, and leave it to dry on paper towels.

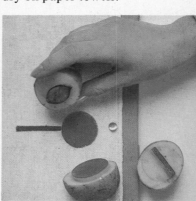

8 Print one shape close to the next one until the motif is complete. Let each layer dry before overprinting.

Potato printing

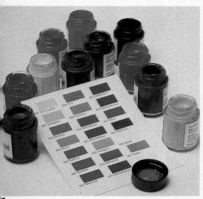

1 Permanent fabric printing colors come in a wide range of shades which will create bright motifs.

2 Assemble all of the working materials. Use large kidney-shaped potatoes for the printing.

3 The motif can be sketched or transferred onto white paper. Draw round it and cut out.

5 Pin the paper design to the flat surface of the potato and cut around it for a cleanly-shaped stamp.

6 For a circle, dig an old film tin into the potato. Cut away the surrounding ring of potato.

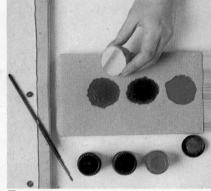

7 Spread paint onto the felt; allow it to be absorbed. Press the stamp onto the felt, then onto the fabric.

Hints

Keep a different stamp for each color, to avoid creating muddy-looking mixtures of colors.

Printing errors: slightly irregular motifs can look just as pretty as very regular ones. Obvious mistakes can be painted with white fabric color and reprinted when dry.

Submerge potato stamps in cold water to keep them fresh. They will keep for one to two days in the refrigerator.

Let freshly-cut stamps dry for a while before beginning to print. Dry stamps print more clearly.

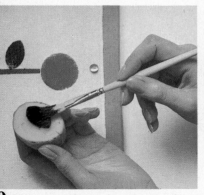

9 You can also print clearly if you paint the color onto the stamp with a paint brush.

10 Press the printed parts on the wrong side with a hot iron. This fixes the color to the fabric.

We arranged the chicks and flowers in a circle for a pretty springtime table but they would also look attractive as a border.

The chicks are all made of simple shapes, cleverly put together.

Making a cheap tablecloth

The tablecloth illustrated here is made of soft white paper. These disposable tablecloths can be bought ready-made in different colors and sizes. They are very cheap so when they get dirty or you become tired of them, you can just throw them away.

To make a circular arrangement, mark the circumference lightly, using a pair of compasses, and work out the position of the motifs before printing to ensure even spacing.

Every member of the family will enjoy printing these colorful motifs onto paper.

Children, especially, lov[e] making gay patterns wit[h] simple shapes, so let the[m] join in. It doesn't matt[er] if they make a mistak[e] because the materia[ls] are so inexpensive tha[t] they can simply begin agai[n].

Other ideas for motifs

The tiny tin shapes used fo[r] making little pastries ar[e] perfect for print motif[s]. Dig them into the flat su[r]face of the potato and cu[t] away the surroundin[g] potato, leaving the shape[s]. Try using potato printing o[n] simple clothes and acces[s]ories such as blouse[s] skirt hems, and scarves.

Index

Index

Notes

Notes

Notes

Notes